The Australian Heritage Cookbook

*A collection of recipes and memories
from Australian kitchens*

LIFETIME DISTRIBUTORS
"The Book People"

The Australian Heritage Cookbook

Published by Murdoch Books Pty Limited.
Murdoch Books Australia
Pier 8/9, 23 Hickson Road, Millers Point NSW 2000
Phone: +61 (0)2 8220 2000 Fax: +61 (0)2 8220 2558

Author: Joy Hayes
Design: Anne Marie Cummins and Justin Thomas
  for Uber Creative
Photography: Phil Wymant
Food Stylist: Ann Creber
Home Economist: Judy Simmons
Editorial Co-ordinator: Anna Goodwin
Production: Monika Vidovic
Project Co-ordinator: Sarah Aitken

Originally published as *Australian Family Circle
Heritage Cookbook*

This edition published in 2005 for Lifetime Distributors.

ISBN 1 74045 627 0

First printed by Sun Fung Offset Binding Company
Limited in 2004. Reprinted 2005. PRINTED IN CHINA

IMPORTANT: Those who might be at risk from the
effects of salmonella poisoning should consult their
doctor with any concerns about eating raw eggs.

Special thanks to Viscopy and the following Art Galleries
for their assistance in the use of paintings reproduced in
this publication – Art Gallery of New South Wales,
National Gallery of Victoria, Melbourne, National
Gallery of Australia, Bathurst Regional Art Gallery.

Right:
John Skinner Prout
1806-1876
*(Bush landscape with waterfall and an
aborigine stalking native animals, New South
Wales, 1860's)*
Oil on canvas 70.5 x 91.4cm
*Purchased under the terms of the Florence
Turner Blake bequest 1976*
Art Gallery of New South Wales

Previous page:
Margaret Preston
1875-1963
Summer
Oil on canvas 51 x 51cm
purchased 1920
Art Gallery of New South Wales

Following page:
Eugene von Guérard
Sydney heads, 1865
Oil on canvas 56 x 94cm
Bequest of Major H.W. Hall 1974
Art Gallery of New South Wales

W. B. Gould 1801–1853
Flower Piece
Oil on canvas 65.8 x 76.8cm
purchased 1956
Art Gallery of New South Wales

Contents

Tom Roberts 1856–1931
*The Golden Fleece: Shearing at
Newstead 1894
Oil on canvas 104 x 158.7cm
purchased 1894
Art Gallery of New South Wales*

Introduction

In a world of fast food, instant meals and eating on the run it is difficult to imagine an era when meal times were relaxed, social occasions.
The pleasures of a leisurely picnic and the enjoyment of a large Sunday roast now seem nothing more than a memory to today's time-starved families.
Tastes have also changed as pre-packed, foil-wrapped sachets replace the market fresh produce that was the hallmark of previous generations of cooks.

Yet, with only a little time and effort, it is possible to once again experience the robust flavours and warm atmosphere that were so characteristic of this bygone culinary era.

The Australian Heritage Cookbook gives a brief account of the history of Australian food and eating habits as they have developed since 1788. It charts the development of recipes from basic settler foods to the more lavish tastes of later years which absorbed tastes and influences from all over the world.

Many recipes have stood the test of time, and several dishes which the early settlers relied upon to keep them going through the hard times, or simply remind them of their home country, can be recreated in a modern kitchen with no loss of flavour. All recipes have been updated to allow for modern cooking methods and ingredients, and have been tested in our kitchens.

Accompanying the recipes and providing added insight into the customs and tastes of the time is a wide selection of Australian paintings, all chosen for their relevance to Australia's culinary history.

The Australian Heritage Cookbook is truly a veritable feast for the senses and will transport you to a world of charm, beauty and good taste.

The First
Hundred Years

Margaret Preston 1875-1963
Adam & Eve in the Garden
of Eden 1950
Gouache stencil on black card
50.1 x 49.5cm
purchased 1950
Art Gallery of New South Wales

The First Hundred Years

Food was in the forefront of Captain Arthur Phillip's mind in 1788 when he ordered one of the first buildings, a bakehouse, to be constructed on the proposed site of Sydney town. The First Fleet of sailing ships had anchored in Botany Bay at 4 am on 20th January, but Phillip selected Sydney Cove as a more suitable spot for settlement because of its shelter and a stream christened the Tank Stream.

Without adequate food and water there was little chance of survival for the remnants of the 1500 people who had set out from Plymouth to establish a penal settlement in Australia. The stark journey of 12,000 miles had taken eight long, hazardous months.

The flotilla consisted of the warships Sirius and Supply, six transports and three store ships. It carried a mixed company of British seamen, soldiers, officials and a wretched collection of 568 male and 191 female convicts, plus nine children, outcasts from the poorest parts of Great Britain. The appetites of these people and their descendants formed the nucleus of the Australian way of eating which developed over the next 200 years. Their longing for the familiar 18th century dishes of their homeland, such as roast beef and Yorkshire pudding, Irish stew, Scotch eggs, Welsh rarebit, steamed suet pudding and treacle tart, were to be realised when the supply ships at last began to service the promised land, agriculture and grazing had developed, and the hungry years were over. The fact that the diet they craved was totally unsuitable for the climate and conditions in which the settlers found themselves was unimportant to them. The nostalgic image transcended common sense, and it seems that knowledge of nutrition, or any inventive cookery skills were sadly lacking among them.

Captain Phillip's cargo had included cattle, sheep, goats, pigs, poultry, seeds and cuttings, and farm tools, as well as food supplies. But the livestock intended for breeding either escaped, died or was slaughtered to feed the starving. The first pitiful crops sown in desperation in this unfriendly soil not surprisingly faded away, and in any case there were only two farmers in the group.

One soldier and 36 convicts had died on the journey. Those who disembarked were debilitated from malnutrition, vitamin-deficiency diseases, fever, dysentery, confinement and hardship. The unskilled convicts, mainly hardened criminals brutalised by their treatment, were totally unfitted for work and disinclined to contribute to their own survival.

The food supplies had been planned to last for two years. They consisted of flour, rice, salt beef and pork, dried peas, oatmeal, butter, cheese and vinegar. For two years there was hardly any fresh meat or familiar fresh fruit or vegetables and for four years, no fresh milk. Flour and grains were weevilly, transported butter and cheese melted and became rancid in the heat. Fish were plentiful but there were no boats and no real desire to build any. Kangaroos and other wild game and birds were hard to catch; unfamiliar fruits and plants were suspect. Governor Phillip's weekly rations for an adult male were: 7lb bread or flour, 7lb salt beef or 4lb salt pork, 2 lb dried peas, 6 oz butter, ½ lb rice.

Phillip built a hospital and a garden on the slopes adjacent to the bakehouse which serviced the marine encampment and the convicts' tent settlement. One

'We are near Australia! Can't you smell the flowers?' But the realities of living there turned into a nightmare for the newcomers.

woman wrote home: *We are comforted with the hopes of a supply of tea from China, and flattered with getting riches when the settlement is complete, and the hemp which the place produces is brought to perfection. Our kingaroo rats are like mutton, but much leaner; and there is a kind of chickweed so much in taste like our spinach that no difference can be discerned. Something like ground ivy is used for tea, but a scarcity of salt and sugar makes our best meals insipid.* [1]

There was rum, of course, to dull their senses and make them forget their misery. It was a fiery spirit distilled from grain in Bengal and often used as barter instead of money. Governor Phillip had tried to control the rum trade, but after his departure in 1792, illicit trading flourished under successive officials and profiteers who became rich on the proceeds as fast as their consumers, convicts and trusties, revelled in drunkenness and depravity.

Meanwhile Governor Phillip and his lieutenants had celebrated Christmas 1788, their first in Australia, with a meal of roast goose, mince pies and Stilton cheese.

The bewildered aborigines who witnessed the strange behaviour and eating habits of these intruders must have wondered why so many of them were starving. The original aboriginal cuisine was perfectly balanced nutritionally for the nomadic family tribes who fished, hunted and gathered their food with nets, harpoons and spears wherever they wandered. But eating flying foxes, snakes, lizards, goannas, bandicoots, possum eggs, rats, caterpillars, witchetty grubs, moths, and crocodiles, dugong, wild roots, grasses, berries and pods didn't appeal to the British. They grudgingly cooked kangaroo, possum, wallaby, wild duck, pigeon and turkey from necessity. But they made no attempt to understand why the aborigines had appeared happy and well-nourished when their Garden of Eden was invaded, and proceeded to kill them off, decimate them with introduced diseases, brutalise them or use them as slaves.

In those days Australia was a land of great forests, soft-footed animals, rich plant life and perfumed flowers. The Australian writer Mary Gilmore, recalled her grandmother telling her that seamen used to say its scent was akin to the Spice Islands', and voyagers would call to one another as their ships approached her shores, 'We are near Australia! Can't you smell the flowers?' But the realities of living there turned into a nightmare for the newcomers.

By 1790, when the notorious Second Fleet landed, weekly rations for the colony's adults had been reduced to 2 ½lb flour, 2 1b pork and 2 1b rice. By that time the colony was close to starvation, the soldiers and convicts alike emaciated and exhausted. Faced with disaster, Governor Phillip had despatched Sirius to Cape Town in October, 1788 for emergency supplies, but after seven months away, her crew returned with only enough to last a further four months.

The situation was desperate, as one man recalled: *The pork and rice were brought with us from England; the pork had been salted between three and four years and every grain of rice was a moving body from the inhabitants lodged within it. We soon left off boiling the pork which had become so old and dry that it shrunk one half in its dimensions when so dressed. Our usual method of cooking was to cut off the daily morsel and toast it on a fork before the fire, catching the drops which fell on a slice of bread or in a saucer of rice. Our flour was the remnant of what was brought from the Cape and was good. Instead of baking it, soldiers and convicts used to boil it up with greens.*

Dismal as the prospect was, things began to improve. In 1810, Dr Joseph Arnold noted that: *a person coming to Sydney Cove would think himself in the midst of a large city; if he dines on shore he finds all the luxury and elegance of the finest English tables.* [2]

Meanwhile, as the colony staggered from its knees, a style of bush cookery began to emerge, forming the basis

---

[1] *Watkin Tench, An account of the Settlement of Port Jackson in New South Wales. London, 1793.*
[2] *Louisa Anne Meredith. Notes and Sketches of NSW during a residence in the Colony. London, 1844.*

Margaret Preston 1875-1963
Black cockatoos c. 1925
Hand coloured woodcut
24.8 x 25.3cm
Australian National Gallery,
Canberra

Margaret Preston 1875-1963
Still Life
Woodcut, hand-coloured
12.7 x 12.5cm
purchased 1976
Art Gallery of New South Wales

of a national diet. Flour, meat, sugar, tea and salt were the commodities. Fried or grilled beef or mutton, damper sometimes spread with golden syrup or 'bullocky's joy', and billy tea with plenty of sugar were the foods, supplemented with plenty of alcohol.

The importation of sheep and cattle, the success of land grants, grazing and agriculture, and the fruits and vegetables produced on the fertile river flats at Parramatta promised happier times. Elizabeth and John Macarthur built Elizabeth Farm at Parramatta in 1792 and conducted a highly successful farming estate there. When Governor Phillip returned home, 7000 acres were allotted to 1200 amateur farmers; 140 were convicts.

Adventurers, squatters, settlers, itinerant bushmen, shearers, timbergetters, whalers and sealers made up a drifting population outside the settlements and towns. Danish dairy experts, Swedes, Yugoslavs, Hungarians, French and German immigrants arrived and began to make their contributions to dairying, food and wine production. But in 1798, most. of the population were still dependent on government rations. In 1803, the first settlers in Hobart were faced with hunger too, but they must have been more industrious and disposed to helping themselves in the more familiar climate. They developed their horticultural, dairying, brewing and meat industries. They farmed, introduced bees, grew pretty gardens, developed orchards and introduced a flourishing weekly market for settlers' produce as well as exporting wheat and many other food commodities to New South Wales. These people also showed more imagination in their cookery and seemed to make the best they could of wild meats. A Tasmanian dish called Grabber Gullen Pie was a hollowed out pumpkin filled with possum meat and baked in the coals. They fried kangaroo tail and called it Pan Jam, made kangaroo pasties, and a dish called Slippery Bob—kangaroo brains in batter, fried in emu fat.

In 1812, when young Maria Macarthur, a daughter of Governor Gidley King, and new wife of Hannibal Macarthur, John Macarthur's nephew, was setting up her household on a grand scale at Parramatta, Sydney was still a village with oak trees and grass on the footpaths and men in cabbage tree hats in the streets. At The Vineyard, the Macarthur estate, there were picnics, boating on the river, walking, jam making parties and in the evening, singing and dancing. One of the six Macarthur daughters recalled: *Necessaries of all kinds were by that time procurable in Sydney. The orders for The Vineyard were for large quantities. We had huge jars some three feet high for rice and raw sugar, etc. Loaves of sugar ranged on shelves, raisins and currants wholesale. Tea came direct in chests from William Leslie in Canton with many other good things, ginger, coffee and chocolate. Bread was baked at home. Dairy produce came from Sydney. A butcher at the farm killed our own sheep, 'good beef could be procured at Parramatta. Fruit and vegetables ad libitum. In the fruit season a large tray was placed on the sideboard in the dining room prepared for any fruit lover through the day.*

The cellar was filled with casks of English beer, and sherry, marsala and port on draught. Lamps were lit with whale oil, wax candles came from England and tallow ones were made on the farm. The maids were Scottish, the menservants English or Indian immigrants. Convicts were used for outdoor work but never allowed to cross the threshold of the house.

Meals were based on Mrs Beeton's cookbook, which was published in England in 1861 by S. O. Beeton. Maria received from her godmother in England, a long letter of advice on household management with menus, recipes and table plans.[3] These were based on the *Service á la Francaise* fashionable at the time, in which all dishes were set out on the table, with some removed and replaced. This custom changed to the more popular *Service á la Russe*, in which dishes were served in successive courses as they are today. Maria's godmother suggested menus for Social Dinners, A Tolerable Sized Party, A Grand Dance, A Sociable Sandwich, Dinner after an Excursion, and other types of meals, as well as a menu for the simple repast shown overleaf.

By 1840, two years before Sydney became a city, it was reported by one visitor that: *There are several good inns in Sydney . . . at about double the expense in a first rate*

> ### A Family Dinner
> ### with 2 or 3 Friends
> ### — or more.
>
> *Boiled Fish*
> *Oyster Sauce*
> *Vegetables • Salad • Vegetables*
> *Plain Butter*
> *Roast Beef*
>
> *Remove the Fish and put on a Dish*
> *of Scotch Collops —*
> *remove the Salad for a Tart.*

English hotel; and whilst you are served with King's Pattern plate and by about half a dozen waiters, you miss many of the common comforts.[4]

In 1843, Thomas Hamblett informed his mother in England by letter: *Today we had for dinner the leg o f a kangaroo, being the first one we have shot. It is very good eating once in a way, but I should not like to live long on it. The parrots make very good pies equal to pigeon but it seems very extravagant to eat such well dressed Ladies and Gents.*

Another dinner party menu reported in a Sydney newspaper society column in 1846, consisted of: *Wallaby tail soup followed by boiled schnapper with oyster sauce, haunch of kangaroo, wonga wonga pigeon with bread sauce,* *and a dessert of plantains, loquats, guavas, mandarins, pomegranates and cherimoyas.*

With the Gold Rush in 1851, the economy began to explode. Adventurers, confidence men, and speculators from all over the world joined the gold hungry population who threw up everything to go to the Victorian goldfields. Among them were thousands of Chinese, either from China or runaways who had been employed as indentured labourers in New South Wales. Industrious and tenacious, many of them began successful market gardens, greengrocers' shops or restaurants, or found work as cooks when gold fever subsided. They introduced us to steamed rice and stir-fried vegetables and are partly responsible for the great Australian fondness for Chinese food which has become part of our culinary heritage.

By 1852, theatres, hotels, restaurants, cafes, clubs, inns and taverns had multiplied, and the road between Sydney and Melbourne, a journey of six days by coach or fifteen on horseback, *was studded with taverns of one class or another,* according to one traveller.

At the end of the first 100 years of colonisation, there was general prosperity as the country moved towards Federation and its first Parliament. But it was still a male community which hadn't changed much for women since 1836, when an Adelaide woman, Mary Thomas, wrote home to her brother in England: *You will realise that housekeeping is no joke here,* probably one of the understatements of the century.

---

[3]*Advice to a Young Lady in the Colonies being a letter sent from Mrs. E of England
to Maria Macarthur in the Colony of New South Wales in 1812. Greenhouse Publications, Pty. Ltd., 1979.*
[4] *Louisa Anne Meredith, Notes and sketches of NSW during a residence in the Colony. London, 1844.*

This small homestead, built on a free land grant of 30 acres given to convict James Ruse in 1789, was one of the first properties established around Sydney and Parramatta.

It was here that vegetables and fruit were cultivated for the colony, and strawberries were grown from offshoots of a single root that Governor Phillip had brought with him. In 1794 the first plough was introduced, and agriculture began.

Then citrus fruits and many varieties of apples and pears from Tasmania and Victoria became available, enabling industrious housewives to make jams and preserves. Our delicious Apple-Marmalade pie, picture page 89, recipe page 88, could well have been a typical dish of the time.

utmeg, Sour cream, Parsley, chopped, Croûtons, method; Peel, remove

nd salt. Pour in just enough water to cover and cook gently, with the l

r food processor with the milks (or push through a sieve and then stir

over and simmer for 5-7 minutes. Serve with a swirl of sour cream a

eparately. 750g (1/2 lb) pumpkin, 1 medium onion, chopped, 1 teaspoo

ream, Parsley, chopped, Croûtons, method; Peel, remove seeds from pu

n just enough water to cover and cook gently, with the lid on, until the

ith the milks (or push through a sieve and then stir in the milk). Retur

r 5-7 minutes. Serve with a swirl of sour cream and a sprinkling of p

emove seeds from pumpkin, and cut into pieces. Put into a saucepan w

Soups

from pumpkin, and cut into pieces. Put into a saucepan with the onic
until the pumpkin is tender. Purée the contents of the pan in a blend.
milk). Return the purée to the saucepan, adding the sugar and nutme
sprinkling of parsley on each bowl and serve a bowl of crisp croûtor
, Water, 2 cups milk, 2 teaspoons sugar, Pinch of grated nutmeg, Sor
, and cut into pieces. Put into a saucepan with the onion and salt. Po
in is tender. Purée the contents of the pan in a blender or food process
urée to the saucepan, adding the sugar and nutmeg. Cover and simm
on each bowl Sour cream, Parsley, chopped, Croûtons, method; Pee
e onion and salt. Pour in just enough water

FRENCH ONION SOUP
Serves 4

INGREDIENTS
500g (1lb) onions
60g (2oz) butter
2 vegetable or chicken
   stock cubes
5 cups water
1 leek, sliced
Pinch dried thyme
2 cloves garlic, crushed
Salt and freshly ground
   black pepper
¼ cup dry white wine
Sliced French bread
250g (8oz) Gruyère or
   Emmenthaler cheese,
   grated

METHOD
Peel onions and slice thinly. Cook very slowly, over a low heat, in the butter until soft and golden. Stir in stock cubes, water, leek, thyme, garlic, salt and pepper to taste.

Simmer, covered, for 25–30 minutes. Stir in wine. Pour into 1 large ovenproof bowl or into individual heatproof bowls. Cover with bread slices and grated cheese.

Bake in a very hot oven until cheese bubbles and becomes golden brown.

CREAM OF PUMPKIN SOUP
Serves 4

INGREDIENTS
750g (1½ lb)
   pumpkin
1 medium onion,
   chopped
1 teaspoon salt
Water
2 cups milk
2 teaspoons sugar
Pinch of grated nutmeg
Sour cream
Parsley, chopped
Croûtons

METHOD
Peel, remove seeds from pumpkin, and cut into pieces. Put into a saucepan with the onion and salt. Pour in just enough water to cover and cook gently, with the lid on, until the pumpkin is tender. Purée the contents of the pan in a blender or food processor with the milks (or push through a sieve and then stir in the milk). Return the purée to the saucepan, adding the sugar and nutmeg. Cover and simmer for 5–7 minutes.

Serve with a swirl of sour cream and a sprinkling of parsley on each bowl and serve a bowl of crisp croûtons separately.

Opposite page: French
Onion Soup

KIDNEY SOUP
Serves 4-6

INGREDIENTS
6 lamb kidneys or
    250g (8oz) ox kidney
60g (2oz) butter
1 small onion, finely
    chopped
1 small carrot, finely
    chopped
5 cups beef stock
1 tablespoon cornflour
    mixed to a paste with
    cold water
Salt and freshly
    ground pepper
4 tablespoons dry sherry
Croûtons (small squares
    of fried bread) to
    garnish

METHOD
Remove skin and fatty core from kidneys, and cut kidneys into thin slices.

Heat the butter in a heavy saucepan, add kidneys and onion, and stir until kidneys are a rich brown. Add carrot and stock, cover, and simmer for 1 hour or until kidneys are very tender.

Strain stock into a clean saucepan, discarding vegetables. Cut kidney slices into small dice and keep ready.

Heat the stock to boiling point, and stir a little into the cornflour mixture. Return this to the saucepan and stir over medium heat until smooth and boiling. Taste for seasoning, add chopped kidneys and sherry, and simmer for 1-2 minutes.

Serve in heated bowls, sprinkled with croûtons.

CHILLED TOMATO SOUP
Serves 4

INGREDIENTS
1 onion, chopped
1kg (2lb) ripe
    tomatoes, peeled
1 clove garlic, crushed
2 tablespoons vegetable
    oil
3 cups vegetable stock
1 teaspoon sugar
Salt and freshly ground
    pepper
1 teaspoon paprika
4 tablespoons boiled rice
Chopped parsley

METHOD
Cook the onion, tomatoes and garlic in the oil for 5 minutes. Pour on the vegetable stock, cover and simmer 10-15 minutes. Place in a blender or food processor and whizz until smooth.

Return to pan and add sugar, salt, pepper and paprika. Bring to boil and simmer 2-3 minutes. Cool and chill. Serve topped with boiled rice and chopped parsley.

MULLIGATAWNY
Serves 6

INGREDIENTS
1kg (2lb) chicken
  pieces, such as thighs,
  drumsticks, breasts
2 tablespoons plain
  flour
2 teaspoons curry
  powder
1 teaspoon turmeric
½ teaspoon ground
  ginger
60g (2oz) butter
6 cloves
12 peppercorns
1 large apple, peeled
  and diced
6 cups chicken stock
2 tablespoons lemon
  juice
½ cup fresh cream
Salt to taste
Boiled rice and chutney
  to serve

METHOD
Wipe chicken pieces with paper towels. Combine flour,
curry powder, turmeric and ginger and rub well into
chicken. Heat the butter in a heavy saucepan, and lightly
brown the chicken on all sides. Add cloves, peppercorns,
apple and stock, bring to the boil, and simmer covered for
1 hour. Remove chicken pieces, and discard peppercorns
and cloves.

  Skin chicken, and cut flesh into small dice. Return to
soup with lemon juice and cream, gently reheat, and add
salt to taste. Serve in heated bowls, with hot boiled rice and
chutney offered separately to stir into the soup.
*NOTE: If you wish, the soup can be whirled in a blender or
food processor for a smoother texture. You might also like to add
other curry accompaniments such as coconut, sultanas, or
chopped peanuts, as well as the rice and chutney.*

VICHYSSOISE
Serves 4

INGREDIENTS
1 leek
2 tablespoons butter
2 onions, chopped
500g (1lb) potatoes,
  sliced
4 cups vegetable stock
Whipped cream
Snipped chives

METHOD
Wash and slice leek and cook in the butter together with
chopped onions until soft, but not brown.

  Stir in sliced potatoes and stock and cook, covered, until
vegetables are tender. Strain and push vegetables through a
sieve. Mix well and chill thoroughly. Top with a spoonful of
whipped cream sprinkled with chives just before serving.

HEARTY PEA SOUP WITH MEAT
Serves 8

INGREDIENTS
1 cup dried green peas
½ cup yellow split peas
6 cups water
3 onions, chopped
500g (1lb) potatoes, diced
1 cup sliced carrots
1 cup diced celery
1kg (2lb) pot roast or half leg of lamb
1 tablespoon whole peppercorns
2 bay leaves
2 teaspoons salt
250g (8oz) shredded cabbage
Chopped parsley

METHOD
Cover peas with cold water and allow to stand overnight. Next day, drain and place in a large saucepan with the 6 cups water.

Add onions, potatoes, carrots, celery, meat, peppercorns, bay leaves and salt. Cover and cook gently 1½ hours. Add shredded cabbage and cook 10 more minutes.

Skim fat from top.

Remove meat from soup and cut into slices. Serve either on a plate with the soup or cut pieces smaller and stir into soup. If desired serve some meat in the soup and maybe serve the remaining meat sliced with mustard or horseradish next day. Sprinkle chopped parsley over soup just before serving.

COCK-A-LEEKIE
Serves 6-8

INGREDIENTS
7 cups chicken stock
6 leeks washed and sliced
Meat from 1 cooked chicken, sliced
Salt and pepper
2 tablespoons chopped parsley

METHOD
Heat chicken stock, stir in leeks and cook gently until tender. Stir in chicken and season well with salt and pepper. Simmer until piping hot, stir in parsley and serve.

Opposite page:
Hearty Pea Soup with
Meat, recipe above.

OXTAIL SOUP
Serves 8

INGREDIENTS
1kg (2lb) oxtail, jointed
10 cups water
Plain flour
Salt and pepper
2 tablespoons butter
125g (4oz) bacon
    pieces, with excess fat
    removed
2 onions, sliced
3 carrots, sliced
¾ cup chopped celery
2 parsley sprigs
1 bay leaf
1 thyme sprig
12 peppercorns
3 tablespoons barley
Chopped parsley

METHOD
Put the oxtail in a saucepan with the water. Bring to the boil, then simmer gently for about 2 hours. Remove the oxtail and pat dry. Chill the stock. Coat the oxtail with flour, which has been seasoned with salt and pepper.

Melt the butter and slowly fry the oxtail until browned. Add the bacon, onions, carrots, and celery and cook over gentle heat until the vegetables are browned. Remove solid fat from the stock and pour over the oxtail and vegetables. Add the parsley, bay leaf, and thyme, tied together, the peppercorns, and salt to taste. Slowly bring to the boil. Skim the surface, cover, and simmer for 1 hour.

Lift the oxtail pieces from the pan. Wash the barley and add to the pan. Remove the oxtail flesh from the bones and return to the pan. Cover and simmer for 1 hour.

Remove the bunch of herbs.

Serve sprinkled with chopped parsley.

BARLEY BROTH
Serves 8

INGREDIENTS
1kg (2lb) neck of
    mutton or lamb,
    chopped
8 cups water
125g (4oz) barley
6 cups chopped
    vegetables, e.g. carrot,
    onion, turnip
Salt and pepper

METHOD
Place neck, water and barley in a saucepan. Cover and cook gently 2 hours.

Add vegetables, salt and pepper and cook until tender. Chop meat and serve in soup.

SCOTCH BROTH
Serves 8-10

INGREDIENTS
1kg (2lb) scrag end of
    lamb or mutton
8 cups water
⅓ cup barley
¾ cup dried peas,
    soaked overnight in
    water
1 bay leaf
Sprig fresh thyme
Salt and pepper
2 leeks, sliced
2 large carrots, diced
1 swede or turnip,
    chopped
2 cups sliced cabbage

METHOD
Place meat, water, barley, drained peas, bay leaf, thyme, salt
and pepper to taste in a large saucepan. Bring to boil and
cook gently 2 hours. Add vegetables and simmer until
tender, about ½ hour. Sprinkle with chopped parsley
when serving.

JELLIED CONSOMMÉ
Serves 6-8

INGREDIENTS
1kg (2lb) mixture beef
    and veal bones
500g (1lb) chicken
    pieces
8 cups water
1 large carrot
1 large onion
Salt and peppercorns
½ cup dry sherry

METHOD
Place bones, chicken, water, whole carrot and unpeeled
onion in a large saucepan.

Add salt and peppercorns to taste, cover with lid and
bring to boil.

Cook gently 3 hours. Strain through a fine sieve and
allow stock to cool. Stir in sherry and taste for seasoning.
Chill and serve in small bowls. Use chicken in any recipe
requiring cooked chicken.

ngredients 500 g (1lb) firm-fleshed fish fillets 13/4 cups water 1 small ce
(4oz) scallops, split into halves 185 g (6oz) small mushrooms, thinly sl
50g (8oz) prawns, shelled and deveined Buttered breadcrumbs method
eat the water with the celery, onion, parsley, bay leaf, and wine un
emove the fish with a slotted spoon and put aside. Add the scallops to
easure and reserve 11/4 cups. Cook the mushrooms and shallots gentl
haped individual ovenproof dishes, or into a shallow ovenproof dish.
he reserved fish stock and cook, stirring until boiling. Simmer for 3-4 r
-3 minutes to reheat. Spoon into the dishes or dish. Top with buttere
edium heat until crisp). Put into a hot oven to reheat.

Fish and Shellfish

alk 1/2 small onion 2 parsley sprigs 1 bay leaf 2/3 cup dry white wine 12
hallots, finely chopped Butter Salt and pepper 1 tablespoon plain flou
e skin from the fish and cut the flesh into small cubes, taking out bone
ing. Simmer for 5 minutes. Add the fish and simmer until just tende
an and simmer for 5 minutes. Remove the scallops and strain the liqui
tter until softened. Add salt and pepper to taste. Spoon into 4-6 shel
tablespoon butter, add the flour, and stir for a minute. Gradually ad
s. Add salt and pepper, then the fish, prawns, and scallops. Simmer fo
bs (about 6 tablespoons tossed in 3 tablespoons of melted butter ove

SAILORS' PIE
Serves 4

INGREDIENTS
1kg (2lb) potatoes
1 x 56g can flat
anchovy fillets, drained
¼ cup grated tasty
   cheese
¼ cup chopped parsley
½ cup sour cream
375g (12oz) whiting
   or flathead fillets
Salt and pepper
250g (8oz) scallops or
   mussels

METHOD
Peel and cook potatoes in boiling salted water until tender.
Drain. Chop anchovies and mix with cheese, parsley and
sour cream.

Place fish fillets on one half of a greased ovenproof dish.
Season with salt and pepper to taste and add the scallops or
mussels. Cover with anchovy mixture.

Press potatoes through a sieve directly into the remaining
half of the dish, next to the fish.

Bake in a moderately hot oven 20-25 minutes until fish
flakes when tested with a fork and top is lightly browned.

SHELLFISH VOL-AU-VENT
Serves 4-5

INGREDIENTS
3 tablespoons butter
1 small leek, thinly sliced
125g (4oz) mushrooms,
   thinly sliced
3 tablespoons flour
1½ cups milk
¼ cup white wine
¼ cup cream
1 egg yolk
½ teaspoon tarragon
Salt and pepper
1 dozen oysters, shelled
1 dozen mussels, shelled
18 or 20cm (7 or 8in)
   vol-au-vent case
Chopped parsley
1 spring onion, finely
 · chopped
Paprika

METHOD
Melt the butter, add the leek and mushrooms and cook
gently until just softened. Sprinkle in the flour, stir a few
minutes then slowly add the milk. Cook, stirring until
thickened.

Stir in the wine and cook over low heat a few more
minutes. Remove from heat.

Beat the cream lightly with the egg yolk and stir slowly
into sauce. Add the tarragon and season with salt and
pepper. Add the oysters and mussels and simmer gently
2-3 minutes.

Meanwhile heat through the pastry case in a moderate
oven. Spoon the shellfish mixture into the case, garnish
with parsley, spring onion and a dusting of paprika.
Serve at once.

Right: Sailors' Pie,
recipe above.

Bernard Hall
1859–1935
The Giant Crab (c.1928)
Oil on canvas 63.6 x 111.8cm
Felton Bequest 1930
National Gallery of Victoria,
Melbourne

LOBSTER THERMIDOR
Serves 4

INGREDIENTS
2 medium lobsters or
  crayfish
1¼ cups milk
1 bay leaf
½ small onion
2 cloves
3 tablespoons butter
2 tablespoons plain flour
Salt
Pinch of cayenne pepper
Pinch of grated nutmeg
4 shallots, chopped
½ cup dry white wine
1¼ cups cream
1 teaspoon French
  mustard
¾ cup grated Swiss
  cheese

METHOD
Halve the lobsters lengthwise, remove the flesh and cut into pieces, reserving the shells. Bring the milk to the boil with the bay leaf, onion, and cloves. Put aside until lukewarm and then strain. Melt half the butter, add the flour, and stir over medium heat for 1–2 minutes without letting it colour. Gradually stir in the warm milk and cook, stirring, until the sauce boils and thickens. Stir in salt to taste, cayenne pepper, and nutmeg. Simmer for 1–2 minutes. Put the lobster shells in a moderate oven to warm. Melt the remaining butter, add the shallots, and cook gently until softened. Add the wine and cook over high heat until reduced by half. Stir in the white sauce, cream, and mustard. Simmer for a minute. Stir in ½ cup of the cheese and simmer until melted. Stir in the lobster meat.

Spoon into the shells, sprinkle with the remaining cheese, and brown under the griller.

SEAFOOD À LA MODE
Serves 8

INGREDIENTS
1½ cups dry white wine
½ cup water
1 bay leaf
500g (1lb) scallops,
  rinsed
750g (1½lb) prawns,
  peeled and deveined
1 small white onion,
  finely chopped
2 tablespoons butter
¼ cup plain flour
½ teaspoon salt
½ cup milk
½ cup cream
8 vol-au-vent cases,
Watercress (optional)
Lemon wedges (optional)

METHOD
Bring the wine to boiling point with the water and bay leaf. Add the scallops and simmer for 3–4 minutes. Drain, reserving the liquid, and mix with the prawns.

Gently fry the onion in the butter until just tender but not browned. Stir the flour and salt in until smooth. Gradually stir in the reserved stock. Cook, stirring, until boiling. Reduce the heat and simmer for 5 minutes. Add the milk, cream, prawns, and scallops.

Stir over low heat until heated through.

Spoon into warmed pastry cases. If you wish, garnish with watercress and lemon.

*Following pages:
Shellfish Vol-au-vent,
recipe page 28*

FISH SOUFFLÉ
Serves 4

INGREDIENTS
500g (1lb) fish fillets
⅓ cup fresh
　breadcrumbs
2 tablespoons milk
2 eggs, separated
½ cup cream
¼ teaspoon dried
　tarragon
Salt
Pinch of cayenne pepper
1 teaspoon French
　mustard

METHOD
Remove the skin and bones and chop the fish coarsely. Put in a saucepan with the breadcrumbs, milk, lightly beaten egg yolks, and cream. Stir over gentle heat for 3-4 minutes. Remove from the heat and beat with a wooden spoon. Add the tarragon, salt to taste, cayenne pepper, and mustard. Beat again for 30 seconds. Beat the egg whites until soft peaks form and fold in.

Turn into a greased 18 cm (7 in) soufflé dish or straight-sided ovenproof dish and bake in a moderate oven for 35-40 minutes.

FISH PARISIENNE
Serves 4-6

INGREDIENTS
500g (1lb) firm-fleshed
fish fillets
1¾ cups water
1 small celery stalk
½ small onion
2 parsley sprigs
1 bay leaf
⅔ cup dry white wine
125g (4oz) scallops, split
into halves
185g (6oz) small
　mushrooms, thinly
　sliced
3 shallots, finely chopped
Butter
Salt and pepper
1 tablespoon plain flour
250g (8oz) prawns,
　shelled and deveined
Buttered breadcrumbs

METHOD
Remove skin from the fish and cut the flesh into small cubes, taking out bones. Heat the water with the celery, onion, parsley, bay leaf, and wine until boiling. Simmer for 5 minutes.

Add the fish and simmer until just tender. Remove the fish with a slotted spoon and put aside. Add the scallops to the pan and simmer for 5 minutes. Remove the scallops and strain the liquid. Measure and reserve 1¼ cups. Cook the mushrooms and shallots gently in butter until softened. Add salt and pepper to taste. Spoon into 4-6 shell-shaped individual ovenproof dishes, or into a shallow ovenproof dish.

Melt 1 tablespoon butter, add the flour, and stir for a minute. Gradually add the reserved fish stock and cook, stirring until boiling. Simmer for 3-4 minutes. Add salt and pepper, then the fish, prawns, and scallops. Simmer for 2-3 minutes to reheat.

Spoon into the dishes or dish. Top with buttered crumbs (about 6 tablespoons tossed in 3 tablespoons of melted butter over medium heat until crisp). Put into a hot oven to reheat.

MR LEE'S STIR-FRY
Serves 1-2

INGREDIENTS
Vegetable oil
1 clove garlic, crushed
2 Chinese cabbage
   leaves, sliced
1 carrot, cut in
   matchsticks
1 small turnip, cut in
   matchsticks
1 white onion, sliced
   lengthwise
4 mushrooms, sliced
2 teaspoons chopped
   fresh coriander or
   ¾ teaspoon dried
1 teaspoon finely
   chopped fresh ginger
   or ½ teaspoon ground
   ginger
1 tablespoon honey and
   1 tablespoon lemon
   juice mixed with a
   little water
12 cooked yabbies or 6
   large cooked prawns
1 tablespoon soy sauce

METHOD
Heat oil in a large heavy frypan or wok. Add garlic. Stir-fry cabbage, carrot, turnip, onion and mushrooms until lightly cooked. Add coriander, ginger, honey and lemon juice and toss quickly to blend flavours. Add yabbies or prawns and soy sauce and toss quickly to heat.

Serve with steamed rice or noodles. Multiply quantities to serve more people as you wish.

SCALLOPS MORNAY
Serves 4

INGREDIENTS
750 g (1½lb) scallops
1 cup dry white wine
60g (2oz) butter
1 small onion, chopped
3 tablespoons flour
Salt and cayenne pepper
1 cup milk
1 cup grated tasty cheese

METHOD
Cook scallops and wine gently 2-3 minutes. Remove and slice. Cook butter and onion 2-3 minutes, stir in flour, salt and pepper and cook 2 minutes.

Add milk and wine from scallops and stir until boiling and thickened. Stir in cheese and scallops. Heat through and serve.

Following pages:
Mr. Lee's Stir-fry,
recipe above.

x 3kg (6lb) goose 21/2 tablespoons plain flour 3 tablespoons brandy 11,
tblespoons butter 1large onion, chopped 2 Granny Smith apples, peelec
f day-old bread, toasted in the oven 2 teaspoons finely grated lemon
aspoon dried thyme Salt and pepper to taste method Make the stuff
ith damp paper towels. Remove the oil sac from the parsonis nose, usir
r secure with poultry pins. Truss the bird, then wipe over with paper t
a lightly oiled baking dish. Put the dish over high heat and sear the b
r 15 minutes. Baste, cover with foil, and reduce the temperature to mo
f the cooking time. Transfer to a heated serving platter, remove th
tblespoons of juice from the pan, add the remaining tablespoon of flou
ir in the stock and cook, stirring, until boiling. Simmer for 2-3 minutes

Poultry

stock made from neck and giblets of goose, or chicken stock Stuffing
d, and diced 1 1/2 cups chopped stoned soft prunes 31/2 cups small cube
1/4 cup chopped parsley 1 teaspoon snipped fresh thyme leaves or 1,
move excess fat from the inside of the goose. Wipe inside and outsid
en scissors. Fill the cavity loosely with the stuffing. Sew up the openir
to dry thoroughly. Sprinkle 1 1/2å tablespoons of the flour over and pu
rm the brandy, set alight, and pour over the goose. Roast in a hot ove
Roast for 21/2 hours, removing the foil about 30 minutes before the er
ing string, and keep warm while you make the gravy. Pour all but
stir over medium heat until browned, scraping up the pan juices. Slow
with the goose. Stuffing: Melt the butter, add the onion, and fry gent

SETTLER'S CHICKEN
Serves 4

INGREDIENTS
1 boiling fowl
5 cups water
1 carrot, sliced
2 stalks celery, sliced
1 onion or leek
2 sprigs parsley
1 onion stuck with
   cloves
Salt to taste

METHOD
Place all ingredients in a large saucepan, including giblets if included.

Cook with lid on over a low heat until tender about 2 hours.

Lift the fowl out and leave the stock to cook a little longer to obtain a stronger flavour.

Skim fat from top. Reserve stock for soups. Serve fowl hot, sliced with parsley sauce or cold with salad.

CHICKEN KIEV
Serves 6

INGREDIENTS
125g (4oz) butter
1 clove garlic, crushed
1 tablespoon lemon juice
2 tablespoons chopped
   parsley
Salt and pepper
3 whole chicken breasts,
   skinned, boned and
   halved
Flour
2 eggs, beaten
Fine dry breadcrumbs
Oil for frying

METHOD
Mix butter, garlic, lemon juice, parsley, salt and pepper together. Shape into a rectangle 5 x 8 cm (2 x 3 in). Chill until firm.

Pound chicken breasts, one piece at a time, between sheets of waxed paper until ½ cm (¼ in) thick, taking care not to tear chicken.

Cut chilled butter into 6 equal finger-sized pieces. Place in centre of chicken, fold in edges and roll up to completely enclose filling. Fasten with a wooden toothpick.

Roll in flour, then dip in beaten eggs and finally roll in the breadcrumbs. Chill 1 hour. This process may be repeated once again if desired.

Heat oil in deep fryer and cook 7–10 minutes until golden brown and completely cooked through. Drain and remove toothpicks. Serve with lightly braised cucumber slices with seeds removed and rice. Garnish with lemon wedges.

Opposite page: Settler's Chicken, recipe above

CREAMY MUSHROOM CHICKEN
Serves 4-5

INGREDIENTS
1kg (2lb) chicken
  pieces
12 small onions
2 tablespoons butter
125g (4oz)
  mushrooms, sliced
2 tablespoons flour
1 cup milk
¾ cup evaporated
  milk or cream
Salt and pepper
125g (4oz) bacon,
  cooked crisp

METHOD
Place chicken pieces, seasoned lightly with salt and
pepper, in a baking dish and bake until brown and tender,
about 30 minutes. Turn now and again to prevent sticking.

Cook onions until almost tender. Drain and then
lightly brown in the butter. Keep hot with the chicken.
Add mushrooms to the same pan in which the onions
were browned, adding a little extra butter if necessary
and cook until lightly browned. Remove.

Stir flour into the mushroom liquid in pan and cook
2-3 minutes. Add milk and cream and stir until
thickened and boiling. Season with salt and pepper and
stir in mushrooms.

Pour over chicken and onions and sprinkle with
crumbled bacon. Mashed pumpkin goes well with
this dish.

CURRIED FOWL
Serves 4-6

INGREDIENTS
2 tablespoons butter
1 cooking apple, peeled,
  cored and chopped
1 onion, chopped
1 tablespoon curry
  powder
1½ cups milk or water
2 tablespoons ground
  rice, blended with
  water
1 tablespoon coconut
Salt
1 cooked fowl,
  chopped, see Settler's
  Chicken, page 40

METHOD
Cook butter, apple, onion and curry powder until soft.

Stir in milk and blended ground rice and cook until
thickened. Add coconut, salt and fowl and cook
15 minutes.

*Opposite page: Creamy
Mushroom Chicken,
recipe above.*

COQ AU VIN
Serves 6

INGREDIENTS
2kg (4lb) chicken
pieces
2 tablespoons flour
seasoned with salt and
pepper
3 tablespoons butter or
ghee
125g (4oz) bacon,
diced
250g (8oz) very small
onions
185g (6oz) button
mushrooms
2 cloves garlic, crushed
½ teaspoon dried
thyme
1 bay leaf
1 bottle red wine

METHOD
Roll chicken pieces in the seasoned flour. Heat butter
or ghee, add chicken and brown all over. Remove from
pan. Add bacon, onions and mushrooms and brown
lightly. Return chicken to pan.

Stir in garlic, thyme, bay leaf and wine. Cover with
tight-fitting lid and cook gently until tender, about 1½
hours.

WINE GLAZED DUCK
Serves 4

INGREDIENTS
1 large duck
Salt
Paprika
Ground ginger
1 small onion, grated
1 cup red wine
⅓ cup brown sugar
1 tablespoon cornflour
¼ teaspoon salt
2 teaspoons grated
lemon rind

METHOD
Cut duck into quarters and remove any excess fat.
Arrange duck pieces in a single layer in a baking dish and
bake uncovered in a preheated hot oven for 30 minutes.

Remove duck from oven and pour off fat that has
accumulated in the dish. Season duck pieces generously
with salt, paprika and ginger and return to the dish.
Sprinkle with the onion, pour in half a cup of the wine,
and cover dish with a lid or aluminium foil.

Continue cooking until duck is tender (about 45
minutes) turning pieces now and then.

In a small saucepan, combine sugar, cornflour, salt,
lemon rind, and remaining half cup of wine. Bring to the
boil, stirring, and simmer until smooth and thickened.
Spoon over duck and bake uncovered for another 10-15
minutes basting often, until duck is glazed.

Vane's Chicken
Watercolour 33 x 37cm
purchased 1918
Art Gallery of New South Wales

ORANGE GARLIC DUCK

Serves 4

INGREDIENTS

1 x 2.25kg (4½lb)
    duck
2 oranges
5 cloves garlic, crushed
Salt
Freshly ground pepper
3 tablespoons butter
1½ cups dry white
    wine
1 teaspoon flour
1 teaspoon butter

METHOD

Remove excess fat from inside the cavity of the duck
and wipe thoroughly with a paper towel. Cut unpeeled
oranges into quarters and fill into duck together with
garlic, salt and pepper. Secure with small skewers.

Melt the 3 tablespoons butter in a large frying pan
and brown duck all over. Remove and cook in a
moderately hot oven directly on the oven grid with a
baking dish underneath on the shelf below. Cook 25
minutes on each thigh side then on the back for
approximately 30 minutes until tender.

When the juices start to drip into the baking dish
gradually stir in the wine and baste the duck with this
several times. When the duck is cooked, there should be
a delicious gravy in the baking dish. Skim off excess fat.
Place baking dish over direct heat and whisk in the 1
teaspoon flour and 1 teaspoon butter blended together.
Stir until thickened and serve with the duck.

PHEASANT WITH APPLES

Serves 4

INGREDIENTS

4 tablespoons butter
1 x 1.5kg (3lb)
    pheasant, trussed
1 large Granny Smith
    apples, peeled, cored
    and sliced
2 teaspoons sugar
1¼ cups cream
1 tablespoon lemon juice
Salt and freshly ground
black pepper

METHOD

Melt half the butter in a large pan. Add pheasant and
brown all over. Remove.

Add remaining butter, apples and sugar and cook
until soft. Place apples in an ovenproof dish, add
pheasant and pour over butter mixture. Cover and bake
in a moderate oven 40 minutes. Pour cream, lemon
juice, salt and pepper over, replace lid and cook until
tender.

Opposite page:
Orange Garlic Duck,
recipe above.

ROAST GOOSE
Serves 6-8

INGREDIENTS

1 x 3kg (6lb) goose
2½ tablespoons plain
   flour
3 tablespoons brandy
1½ cups stock made
   from neck and giblets
   of goose, or chicken
   stock

Stuffing
2 tablespoons butter 1
   large onion, chopped
2 Granny Smith apples,
   peeled, cored, and
   diced
1½ cups chopped
   stoned soft prunes
3½ cups small cubes
   of day-old bread,
   toasted in the oven
2 teaspoons finely
   grated lemon rind
¼ cup chopped parsley
1 teaspoon snipped
   fresh thyme leaves or
   ½ teaspoon dried
   thyme
Salt and pepper to taste

METHOD

Make the stuffing. Remove excess fat from the inside of the goose. Wipe inside and outside with damp paper towels. Remove the oil sac from the parson's nose, using kitchen scissors. Fill the cavity loosely with the stuffing. Sew up the opening or secure with poultry pins. Truss the bird, then wipe over with paper towels to dry thoroughly. Sprinkle 1 ½ tablespoons of the flour over and put in a lightly oiled baking dish. Put the dish over high heat and sear the bird. Warm the brandy, set alight, and pour over the goose. Roast in a hot oven for 15 minutes. Baste, cover with foil, and reduce the temperature to moderate.

Roast for 2½ hours, removing the foil about 30 minutes before the end of the cooking time.

Transfer to a heated serving platter, remove the trussing string, and keep warm while you make the gravy.

Pour all but 2 tablespoons of juice from the pan, add the remaining tablespoon of flour, and stir over medium heat until browned, scraping up the pan juices. Slowly stir in the stock and cook, stirring, until boiling. Simmer for 2-3 minutes. Serve with the goose.

Stuffing: Melt the butter, add the onion, and fry gently until softened. Add the apples and cook for 2 minutes, stirring constantly. Transfer to a bowl and mix in all remaining ingredients.

DUCK WITH FRUIT STUFFING
Serves 4

INGREDIENTS
1 x 2kg (4lb) duck
Softened butter
Juice of ½ medium
  lemon
½ cup orange juice
1 teaspoon gelatine
Salt and pepper

Stuffing
¾ cup chopped raisins
¼ cup chopped stoned
  prunes
2 medium onions, grated
1 large orange, peeled
  and finely chopped
Salt and pepper
2 cups soft fresh
  breadcrumbs
½ teaspoon dried
  marjoram
1 tablespoon finely
  grated lemon rind
1 tablespoon melted
  butter

METHOD
Make the stuffing and fill the duck. Close the opening with small skewers or poultry pins. Truss and put in a greased baking dish. Rub softened butter over the duck and cover loosely with foil, making sure it does not touch the bird. Bake in a moderate oven for 1 ½ hours. Remove foil and continue baking for 30 minutes, or until tender, basting occasionally with the pan juices. Remove from the dish and allow to cool before chilling in the refrigerator.

Heat the fruit juices, sprinkle the gelatine over, add salt and pepper, and stir until the gelatine has dissolved. Chill until the mixture has the consistency of unbeaten egg white. Brush over the duck and put in the refrigerator to set. Brush with the remaining fruit glaze and chill again until set.

Stuffing: Pour boiling water over the raisins and prunes. Leave for 10 minutes and then drain thoroughly. Mix the onions with the orange, salt and pepper, breadcrumbs, marjoram, lemon rind, raisins and prunes, and melted butter.

Ingredients 1 x 2.5kg (5lb) leg of lamb 90g (3oz) butter 1 medium onion
chopped fresh rosemary (or 1/2 teaspoon dried) 2 teaspoons chopped f
round pepper Gravy 11/2 tablespoons plain flour 11/2 cups stock made
one. Heat the butter and fry onion until soft and golden. Skin and c
rowned. Remove from heat and add breadcrumbs, herbs and salt and p
ith string. Season with salt and pepper, arrange on a greased rack i
bout 2 hours for well done lamb, basting now and then with juices th
arving.Gravy: Pour off all but 2 tablespoons of drippings in pan, an
ontinue stirring until gravy is smooth and thickened. Taste for season
utter 1 medium onion, finely chopped 2 lamb kidneys 2 cups soft, whi
easpoons chopped fresh sage (or 1/2 teaspoon dried) 2 teaspoons chop

Meat & game

chopped 2 lamb kidneys 2 cups soft, white breadcrumbs 2 teaspoon
ge (or 1/2 teaspoon dried) 2 teaspoons chopped parsley Salt and fine
mb bone method Ask the butcher to bone the lamb for you and save th
kidneys and cut into small dice. Add to the pan and stir until light
o taste. Allow to cool a little, then stuff lamb and tie into a neat shap
ing dish, and place in a preheated moderate oven.Roast uncovered f
ct in the pan. Allow to rest for 20 minutes before removing string ar
n flour over low heat. When well blended, gradually stir in stock ar
strain into a gravy boat. ingredients 1 x 2.5kg (5lb) leg of lamb 90g (30
dcrumbs 2 teaspoons chopped fresh rosemary (or 1/2 teaspoon dried)
rsley Salt and finely ground pepper Gravy 11/2 tablespoons plain flo

SHEARERS' STEW WITH DUMPLINGS
Serves 6 hungry shearers or 8 people

INGREDIENTS
1 tablespoon oil
1 tablespoon butter
1kg (2lb) chopped
   mutton or two-tooth
   lamb, rolled in
   seasoned flour
3 onions, quartered
3 parsnips, thickly sliced
3 carrots, thickly sliced
2 sticks celery, chopped
Meat or vegetable stock
   or water
3 tablespoons chopped
   parsley
¾ teaspoon mixed
   herbs
1 tablespoon
   Worcestershire sauce
Salt, pepper and a pinch
   of sugar

METHOD
Heat oil and butter in a large heavy frypan and brown meat, adding a little extra oil if necessary. Push to one side and sauté onions until transparent. Transfer to a heavy stewpan, adding bits left in bottom of frypan blended with a little stock or water. Add parsnips, carrots and celery and sufficient stock or water to barely cover, along with parsley, herbs, Worcestershire sauce, salt, pepper and sugar. Simmer about 2 hours or until meat is tender, on low heat. Serve with Jumbuck Dumplings.

JUMBUCK DUMPLINGS

INGREDIENTS
2 cups self raising flour
1 tablespoon chopped
   parsley
Salt and plenty of black
   pepper
About ¾ cup milk
   or water

METHOD
Put flour, parsley, salt and pepper in a bowl and stir in milk or water until dough forms a soft dropping consistency. With floury palms lightly roll mixture into balls and place on top of stew while it is simmering. Cover and cook, about 15 minutes before ready to serve stew.

*Opposite page:
Shearers' Stew with
Jumbuck Dumplings,
recipe above*

PARSNIP CAKES

INGREDIENTS
4 medium parsnips,
  cooked and mashed
4 tablespoons
  self-raising flour
1 egg, beaten
Salt, pepper and dash of
  nutmeg
Butter for frying

METHOD
Mix mashed parsnips with flour, egg, salt, pepper and nutmeg. Form into cakes with floury hands and fry on both sides in butter until brown and crisp. Drain on kitchen paper.

OXTAIL STEW
Serves 4

INGREDIENTS
2 large oxtails, jointed
Plain flour
Salt and pepper
2 tablespoons oil
2 onions, sliced
1 cup water
1 cup claret
3 large tomatoes, peeled
  and chopped
4 cloves
4 carrots, sliced
1 cup sliced celery
1 turnip or parsnip,
  cubed

METHOD
Coat the oxtails with the flour seasoned with salt and pepper. Heat the oil, add the oxtails, and brown slowly all over. Add the onions and fry until softened. Pour the fat from the pan.

Add the water, claret, tomatoes, and cloves. Stir until boiling, scraping up the pan juices. Cover and simmer for 1 1/2 hours.

Cool and then chill in the refrigerator overnight. Remove the fat from the top, return to the saucepan, and add the vegetables. Cover and simmer 1 hour, or until tender.

ABERDEEN SAUSAGE
Serves 6-8

INGREDIENTS
500g (1lb) lean
  minced steak
250g (8oz) bacon,
  minced
1 cup soft breadcrumbs
Dash of tomato or
  Worcestershire sauce
  (or both)
1 teaspoon grated
  lemon peel
1 teaspoon mixed herbs
1 tablespoon chopped
  parsley
Pepper and salt
1 egg
2 hard-boiled eggs
Dry breadcrumbs

METHOD
In a bowl mix together all ingredients, except hard-boiled eggs and dry breadcrumbs.

    Form into a roll. Make a pocket along centre and place hard-boiled eggs lengthwise in it.

    Cover with mixture. Flour sausage well and tie in a floured cloth. Boil gently 2 hours.

    While hot, carefully remove from cloth. Chill overnight. Roll in dry breadcrumbs before serving.

    Serve sliced, with salads. This makes a great buffet dish.

PORK STROGANOFF
Serves 4

INGREDIENTS
750g (1½ lb) pork
  shoulder
2 tablespoons butter
3 onions, sliced
Salt and pepper
1 cup beef stock
2 tablespoons tomato
  paste
1 cup sour cream
2 teaspoons soy sauce

METHOD
Cut pork into strips. Melt butter and quickly brown pork all over. Add onions, salt and pepper and cook until browned. Stir in beef stock and tomato paste. Cover with a tight fitting lid and cook gently until tender, about 25 minutes.

    Stir in sour cream and soy sauce and reheat gently. Serve with rice and crusty bread.

Following pages: Plum glazed corned beef, recipe page 59, with parsnip cakes, recipe page 54.

Frederick McCubbin
1855-1917

*Girl with bird at the King
Street bakery, 1886*
Oil on canvas 40.7 x 46cm
purchased 1969
*National Gallery of Australia,
Canberra*

At the time of this painting,
Melbourne was a colourful,
raffish city still recovering from
gold mania. It had a floating
population of criminals, thieves,
ruffians, drunks and itinerant
workers as well as a large
Chinese quarter and a
permanent settlement of
industrious, respectable people,
including about 2,000 young
sewing girls and milliners'
apprentices. This little girl sits
on the cobbled backyard of a
modest cottage in a street which
is now one of the city's most
dignified thoroughfares. Her
meals would have been of the
most basic kind reflecting her
parents' British background.

On Christmas Day, if they
could afford it, the family would
probably sit down to a heavy
meal of roast turkey or chicken,
plum pudding and mince tarts,
even if the temperature was
unbearably hot.

PLUM GLAZED CORNED BEEF
Serves 4-8

INGREDIENTS
1.5kg (3lb) corned
    silverside
1 tablespoon brown
    sugar
1 tablespoon vinegar
1 clove garlic, sliced
1 onion studded with
    4 cloves
4 peppercorns
1 bouquet garni (1 bay
    leaf, sprigs of thyme
    and parsley)
4 carrots
4 small onions, peeled
4 potatoes
4 medium parsnips
1 cup bottled plum sauce
1 teaspoon honey
1 tablespoon orange
    juice

METHOD
Put the corned beef in a heavy saucepan with the brown
sugar, vinegar, garlic, onion with cloves, peppercorns and
bouquet garni. Add enough water to cover. Heat until
boiling, cover and simmer 40 minutes. Add the carrots,
onions, potatoes and parsnips.

Simmer approximately 1 hour longer or until meat is
tender. Remove vegetables when cooked, drain and keep
warm. Reserve parsnips.

Meanwhile melt the plum sauce, honey and orange juice
over hot water, blend and keep warm.

Transfer meat to a heated platter and brush with the
plum glaze. Serve meat sliced and surrounded by vegetables,
with Parsnip Cakes made from reserved parsnips. A green
vegetable and mustard or horseradish sauce go well with
this dish.

GENTLEMAN'S BREAKFAST
(BUBBLE AND SQUEAK)
Serves 1

METHOD
Fry about 1 cup cubed or shredded cold corned beef in
1 tablespoon heated butter with chopped leftover
vegetables, including Parsnip Cakes (about 1 cup
altogether), and season with salt and pepper. Press
mixture into pan and turn until browned on both sides
and formed into a cake.

Place 1 fried egg on top. Sprinkle with chopped parsley
and serve with a selection of bottled sauces.

Cooked cold cabbage and potatoes may be fried with
corned beef instead of leftover vegetables, as in the Irish
dish called Colcannon or as it is known in England,
Bubble and Squeak.

*Following pages:
Gentleman's Breakfast, is
a version of Bubble and
Squeak, and is made from
cold Plum Glazed Corned
Beef, leftover vegetables
and Parsnip Cakes,
recipes. Recipe above.*

PORK MADEIRA
Serves 6

INGREDIENTS
1kg (2lb) pork fillets
2 tablespoons flour
Salt
Freshly ground pepper
2 tablespoons vegetable
   oil
1 tablespoon butter
1 onion, chopped
375g (12oz) button
   mushrooms
2 tablespoons butter,
   extra
½ cup unsweetened
   apple juice
½ cup thickened cream
½ cup Madeira
1 tablespoon tomato
   paste

METHOD
Cut pork into thick pieces and toss in the flour, seasoned with salt and pepper.

Heat oil and 1 tablespoon of butter together, add onion and cook slowly until just changing colour. Stir in mushrooms and cook a few more minutes. Remove onion and mushrooms from pan.

Heat the extra butter, add pork and cook quickly 7–10 minutes. Stir in onion and mushrooms and cook for 1 minute.

Add apple juice, cream, Madeira and tomato paste and stir until thickened and very hot.

Serve with rice or potatoes and salad.

BLANQUETTE DE VEAU
Serves 4

INGREDIENTS
1kg (2lb) diced veal
1 onion, studded with 4
   whole cloves
1 strip lemon peel
2 cloves garlic, crushed
½ cup sliced celery
1 carrot, sliced
1 bay leaf
2 cups dry white wine
½ cup cream
2 tablespoons dry
   vermouth

METHOD
Place meat in a saucepan, add onion studded with the cloves, lemon peel, garlic, celery, carrot, bay leaf and wine. Cover and simmer until tender, about 1 hour.

Remove meat from stock, remove cloves and purÈe stock and vegetables together. Taste for seasoning and return to saucepan. Stir in cream and vermouth and cook until required thickness.

Return meat to sauce and heat through gently. Serve with creamy mashed potato or hot boiled rice.

PORK CHOPS WITH APPLES
Serves 4

INGREDIENTS
4 pork loin chops Salt
  and pepper
1 tablespoon fresh
  thyme
2 tablespoons apple
  cider
4 apples
1 cup apple cider
Salt and pepper
½ cup whipped cream

METHOD
Make several cuts in the fat around edge of chops. Cook in
a frypan until brown on both sides, adding a little oil only if
necessary. Season with salt, pepper and thyme.
Pour over the 2 tablespoons cider.

Peel, halve and core apples. Poach for a few minutes in
the 1 cup of cider. Make cuts in 4 of the apple halves 5 mm
(¼ in) apart, taking care not to cut right through.

Remove chops from pan and place in a heatproof dish.
Place a sliced apple half on top.

Cut the remaining apples in chunks and purÈe in a
blender with the apple cooking liquid and any liquid or
scrapings from the frypan. Season with salt and pepper. Pour
around the chops.

Spoon some whipped cream over the apples and grill
under a medium heat until apples begin to brown.

MELBOURNE GRILL
Serves 4

INGREDIENTS
4 bacon rashers
4 lamb loin chops,
  trimmed
4 thick slices fillet, or
  Scotch fillet or small

4 sausages, parboiled
2 large firm tomatoes,
  halved crosswise
Melted butter
4 lamb kidneys, skinned
  and halved
8 large mushrooms
Salt and freshly ground
  pepper

METHOD
Fry bacon, chops, steaks, sausages and tomatoes on grill and
cook until brown.

Turn over, add kidneys with cores removed and
mushrooms brushed with melted butter.

Turn kidneys after 2 minutes. When cooked, season with
salt and pepper and serve on heated plates.

Chops and steaks can be topped with butter. Serve with
chips or mashed potato, green vegetable or salad.

RICH CASSEROLE OF BEEF
Serves 4

INGREDIENTS
750g (1½lb) chuck
  steak, cubed
2 tablespoons plain flour
Salt and pepper
2-3 tablespoons oil
1 cup red wine
1 bay leaf
1 teaspoon fresh thyme
1 clove garlic, crushed
2 tablespoons tomato
  paste
1 teaspoon juniper
  berries, optional
12 small onions
2 carrots, sliced
1 stalk celery, sliced
1 leek, sliced

METHOD
Toss meat in the flour seasoned with salt and pepper and coat evenly. Brown in the hot oil all over and transfer to an ovenproof dish.

Stir wine into the pan, scraping well to mix in any flour or brown pieces left in the bottom. Add bay leaf, thyme, garlic, tomato paste and juniper berries. Mix well and pour over meat. Cover with lid and cook gently in a moderate oven 1 hour. Add onions, carrots and celery and cook another 30 minutes. Add leeks and cook until meat is tender, about 20-30 minutes.

PIG'S TROTTERS IN RED WINE
Serves 4

INGREDIENTS
6-8 pig's trotters
Salt and freshy ground
  black pepper
2 tablespoons butter
1 leek, washed and sliced
1 cup sliced celery
1 cup sliced carrot
1 onion, studded with
  4 whole cloves
1½ cups red wine
3 cloves garlic, crushed
2 tomatoes, peeled and
  sliced
1 teaspoon fresh thyme
1 teaspoon fresh
  rosemary
1 teaspoon fresh tarragon

METHOD
Season meat with the salt and pepper and brown all over in the butter. Add leek, celery, carrot and the onion studded with the cloves. SautÈ for a few minutes.

Pour over the wine, add garlic, sliced tomato, thyme, rosemary and tarragon. Bring to the boil, cover with lid and cook until tender, about 1½ hours.

Opposite page:
Rich Casserole of Beef,
recipe above.

COLONIAL GOOSE
Serves 6

INGREDIENTS
1 x 2.5kg (5lb) leg
 of lamb
90g (3oz) butter
1 medium onion, finely
 chopped
2 lamb kidneys
2 cups soft, white
 breadcrumbs
2 teaspoons chopped
 fresh rosemary (or
 ½ teaspoon dried)
2 teaspoons chopped
 fresh sage (or
 ½ teaspoon dried)
2 teaspoons chopped
 parsley
Salt and finely ground
 pepper

Gravy
1½ tablespoons plain
 flour
1½ cups stock made
 with lamb bone

METHOD
Ask the butcher to bone the lamb for you and save the
bone. Heat the butter and fry onion until soft and golden.
Skin and core the kidneys and cut into small dice. Add to
the pan and stir until lightly browned. Remove from heat
and add breadcrumbs, herbs and salt and pepper to taste.
Allow to cool a little, then stuff lamb and tie into a neat
shape with string. Season with salt and pepper, arrange on a
greased rack in a baking dish, and place in a preheated
moderate oven.

Roast uncovered for about 2 hours for well done lamb,
basting now and then with juices that collect in the pan.
Allow to rest for 20 minutes before removing string and
carving.

Gravy: Pour off all but 2 tablespoons of drippings in pan,
and stir in flour over low heat. When well blended,
gradually stir in stock and continue stirring until gravy is
smooth and thickened. Taste for seasoning and strain into a
gravy boat.

IRISH STEW
Serves 6

INGREDIENTS
1kg (2lb) lamb
 stewing chops
1.5kg (3lb) potatoes,
 peeled
500g (1lb) onions,
 sliced thickly
Salt and pepper
2½ cups water

METHOD
Trim chops. Slice ¼ of the potatoes and halve the rest. Place
sliced potatoes in a deep saucepan, add chops then the
potato halves.

Season with salt and pepper and pour over the water.
Cover with a tight-fitting lid and cook gently for about 2
hours until chops are tender.

SAVOURY BEEF OLIVES
Serves 4-5

INGREDIENTS
500g (1lb) very thin
  sliced beef (4 slices)
½ cup soft
  breadcrumbs
2 tablespoons chopped
  parsley
1 small apple, peeled
  and chopped
1 bacon rasher, chopped
½ teaspoon dried
  mixed herbs
Salt and pepper
2 tablespoons seasoned
  flour
2 tablespoons vegetable
  oil
2 large carrots, sliced
1 large onion, sliced
1½ cups beef stock
2 tablespoons tomato
  paste
1 bay leaf

METHOD
Trim steak if necessary and cut into 10 cm (4 in) squares.
Combine breadcrumbs, parsley, apple, bacon, herbs, salt and
pepper to taste. Divide between the meat slices, roll up and
secure with strong cotton. Roll in the seasoned flour.

  Heat the oil and brown meat rolls all over. Place in a
greased ovenproof dish together with carrots and onion and
sprinkle over any remaining flour.

  Mix together beef stock and tomato paste. Add bay leaf
and pour into dish. Cover and bake in a moderately slow
oven 1-1¼ hours until tender. Remove cotton before
serving.

HAM FLORENTINE
Serves 4

INGREDIENTS
1 bunch spinach
½ teaspoon nutmeg
4 ham steaks
1½ cups grated tasty
  cheese
1 cup evaporated milk
½ cup milk
2 teaspoons cornflour

METHOD
Wash spinach leaves thoroughly under cold running water.
Cook in a small amount of boiling salted water until tender,
about 10 minutes. Drain and press out as much liquid as
possible.

  Place spinach in a greased ovenproof dish and sprinkle
with the nutmeg. Add the ham steaks cut in half.
Place cheese and milks in a saucepan and stir over a low
heat until cheese melts.

  Blend cornflour with a little cold water, stir into cheese
mixture and simmer 2-3 minutes.

  Pour over ham and bake in a hot oven 20-25 minutes.

W. B. McInnes
Still Life, [date unknown]
Oil on canvas 43.3 x 58.5cm
Gift of Mr A.H. Batwell and Mrs
V.A. Ure Smith 1946
Art Gallery of New South Wales

RABBIT CASSEROLE
Serves 4

INGREDIENTS

1 rabbit, cut into
serving pieces
2 teaspoons vinegar
Plain flour seasoned
with salt and pepper
1 tablespoon oil
1 tablespoon butter
3 medium onions,
coarsely chopped
3 rashers streaky bacon,
diced
1 tablespoon plain flour
1 cup dry white wine
½ cup chicken stock
1 tablespoon tomato
paste
2 sprigs parsley
1 sprig thyme
1 bay leaf
Salt and freshly ground
pepper
125g (4oz) button
mushrooms, halved or
sliced
1 tablespoon extra
butter
Chopped parsley to
garnish

METHOD

Soak rabbit for 6-8 hours in cold salted water with the
vinegar added. Drain pieces and dry thoroughly, then coat
with seasoned flour.

Heat together oil and butter, add the rabbit pieces and
brown all over. Transfer rabbit to an ovenproof dish. Add
onions and bacon to the pan and gently fry until onions
have softened. Add the flour, stir for a minute or two, then
pour in the wine and chicken stock. Add the tomato paste
and stir until boiling. Pour over rabbit in dish, add the
parsley, thyme and bay leaf, tied together, with salt and
pepper to taste.

Cover and cook in a moderately slow oven for about
1½ hours, or until tender. Just before cooking time is
finished, quickly fry the mushrooms in extra butter for a
minute or two and mix into the casserole. Remove bundle
of herbs and serve casserole garnished with chopped parsley.

eggs, separated 1/2 cup caster sugar 1 cup milk, heated 3 teaspoons

mon Sauce 1 egg yolk 1/4 cup sugar 60 g (2oz) butter, softened 2 teasp

d sugar together. Add hot milk and stir thoroughly. Pour into a sa

latine and stir until dissolved. Pour into a bowl and stir over chilled u

til thick. Fold both into orange mixture until evenly mixed. Pour in

voured with orange brandy liqueur and chilled thoroughly, and lemo

Puddings

e, softened in a little water 1 cup orange juice 1 x 300 ml carton crea
ornflour 1/2 cup orange juice 1/4 cup lemon juice method Beat egg yol
and stir over a low heat until hot and almost boiling. Add softene
ntil cold. Stir in orange juice. Beat egg whites until stiff and whip crea
ass serving dish and chill thoroughly. Serve with peeled orange slic
e. Lemon sauce: Place all ingredients in a saucepan and whisk togeth

LIQUEUR SOUFFLÈ
Serves 6

INGREDIENTS
⅓ cup caster sugar
1½ tablespoons plain
   flour
¾ cup milk
¼ cup Orange CuraÁao
1 tablespoon butter
5 egg yolks, beaten
7 egg whites
Pinch salt

METHOD
Stir sugar and flour together in a saucepan. Gradually add milk and stir over a low heat until boiling and thickened.

Remove from heat, stir in liqueur and butter. Pour a little of the hot mixture onto the beaten yolks, stirring well. Return all to saucepan and beat until evenly mixed.

Beat egg whites with a pinch of salt until thick and gently fold into yolk mixture. Pour into a greased (and lightly sprinkled with sugar) 6-cup soufflÈ dish. Bake in a moderately hot oven 35–40 minutes until outside is firm and inside creamy. Serve immediately with top sprinkled with sifted icing sugar.

PEARS BELLE HÈLËNE
Serves 4

INGREDIENTS
2 cups water
¾ cup sugar
Strip of orange rind,
   with pith removed
4 medium, firm pears

Chocolate Sauce
⅔ cup water
2 tablespoons sugar
90g (3oz) plain dark
   chocolate, chopped

METHOD
Heat the water with the sugar, stirring until the sugar has dissolved. Simmer until syrupy and add the orange rind. Peel the pears and core from the base (leave the stalks on).

Add the pears to the syrup, cover, and cook gently until just tender. Leave in the syrup until cold. Drain the pears thoroughly, stand each upright in an individual bowl, or on a serving plate, and spoon some of the chocolate sauce over each.

Chocolate sauce: Put the water and sugar in a saucepan and heat, stirring until the sugar has dissolved. Simmer the syrup for 3–4 minutes. Put the chocolate in a bowl and melt over a saucepan of hot water, stirring occasionally. Pour off the water from the saucepan and add the melted chocolate. Beat in the syrup, a little at a time, using a wooden spoon.

Simmer, stirring, until a thick syrup forms.

Opposite page: Liqueur Souffle, recipe above.

QUEEN OF PUDDINGS
Serves 6-8

INGREDIENTS
1 cup soft, white
   breadcrumbs
2 cups milk, scalded
2 eggs, separated
⅓ cup sugar
3 tablespoons strawberry
   jam
1 cup sliced strawberries

METHOD
Place breadcrumbs in a bowl with hot milk and let stand for 10 minutes. Beat egg yolks with half the sugar and stir into crumb mixture.

Spoon custard into a greased ovenproof dish and bake in a moderately slow oven for 45 minutes, or until firm to the touch.

Combine strawberry jam and sliced strawberries and spread over custard. Whip egg whites until stiff, then beat in remaining sugar to form a meringue.

Swirl meringue over top. Increase oven temperature to moderately hot, and bake pudding for 8-10 minutes, or until meringue is set and lightly browned. Serve hot or warm, by itself or with pouring cream.

SAGO PLUM PUDDING
Serves 4

INGREDIENTS
½ cup sago
1 cup milk
1 cup soft breadcrumbs
1 cup raisins
½ cup sugar
¼ teaspoon bicarbonate
   of soda
2 tablespoons butter,
   melted
A little extra milk, if
   needed

Sweet White Sauce
(recipe follows)

METHOD
Place sago and milk in a large bowl and soak overnight.

Mix in remaining ingredients, adding a little more milk if necessary, to a dropping consistency.

Turn mixture into a greased 6-cup basin, cover with lid or greased foil and steam for 3 hours.

Unmould on to a serving plate and serve with Sweet White Sauce.

Sweet white sauce: Mix 3 teaspoons cornflour, pinch of salt, 1 tablespoon sugar and 1 tablespoon melted butter in a saucepan. Add 1 cup milk little by little, stirring until smoothly blended. Place over moderate heat and stir constantly until boiling. Simmer very gently for 5 minutes, then add 1 teaspoon of vanilla essence. Serve hot.

OLD ENGLISH TRIFLE
Serves 6

INGREDIENTS
1 x 20 cm (8 in)
   sponge cake
Apricot or raspberry jam
½ cup sherry
¼ cup brandy
2½ cups vanilla custard
½ cup toasted chopped
   almonds
Whipped cream
Strawberries

METHOD
Slice cake and spread with jam. Place in a glass dish. Pour over sherry, brandy and lastly custard and chill thoroughly. Sprinkle toasted almonds on top and decorate with cream and strawberries.

PEARS IN CLARET
Serves 4

INGREDIENTS
2 cups claret
1 tablespoon lemon
   juice
1 tablespoon orange
   juice
¼ cup sugar
1 stick cinnamon
4 pears

METHOD
Place claret, lemon juice, orange juice, sugar and cinnamon in a saucepan and heat gently.

Peel pears without removing stems and add to wine syrup.

Cook gently until pears are soft when tested with the point of a sharp knife.

Reduce liquid if necessary after removing pears. Replace pears and leave until cooled.

Serve with whipped cream.

ORANGE SNOW WITH LEMON SAUCE
Serves 8-10

INGREDIENTS
3 eggs, separated
½ cup caster sugar
1 cup milk, heated
3 teaspoons gelatine,
    softened in a little
water
1 cup orange juice
1 x 300ml carton cream

Lemon Sauce
1 egg yolk
¼ cup sugar
60g (2oz) butter,
    softened
2 teaspoons cornflour
½ cup orange juice
¼ cup lemon juice

METHOD
Beat egg yolks and sugar together. Add hot milk and stir thoroughly. Pour into a saucepan and stir over a low heat until hot and almost boiling. Add softened gelatine and stir until dissolved.

Pour into a bowl and stir over chilled water until cold. Stir in orange juice. Beat egg whites until stiff and whip cream until thick. Fold both into orange mixture until evenly mixed.

Pour into a glass serving dish and chill thoroughly. Serve with peeled orange slices flavoured with orange brandy liqueur and chilled thoroughly, and lemon sauce.

Lemon sauce: Place all ingredients in a saucepan and whisk together thoroughly.

Stir over a low heat until thickened and boiling. Stir over chilled water until cold. If sauce thickens too much for pouring, thin down with a little cream.

LEMON SHERRY MOULD
Serves 4-5

INGREDIENTS
1 tablespoon gelatine
¼ cup lemon juice
3 egg whites
¾ cup caster sugar
¾ cup cream, whipped
Grated rind 1 lemon
¼ cup sherry

METHOD
Soften gelatine in the lemon juice in a heatproof cup and stir over hot water until dissolved.

Cool until just starting to thicken.

Beat egg whites until thick, gradually add sugar and beat until thick like meringue.

Fold in whipped cream, lemon rind, sherry and gelatine mixture.

Pour into a wet or lightly oiled 5-cup mould and chill overnight. Unmould onto a serving plate and top and surround with berries or seedless grapes.

Opposite page: Orange Snow with Lemon Sauce, recipe above.

APPLES MARZIPAN
Serves 4-5

INGREDIENTS
4 cooking apples
½ cup water
¼ cup sugar
1 x 200g roll marzipan, grated
2 eggs

METHOD
Peel, core and cut apples into wedges. Stir water and sugar together over a low heat until boiling. Add apples, cover with tight-fitting lid and cook 5-7 minutes, until still slightly firm.

Drain and place in a greased ovenproof dish.

Beat grated marzipan and eggs together in an electric mixer until thick and creamy. Pour over apples and bake in a hot oven 20 minutes until golden brown.

Serve with custard or ice-cream.

BREAD AND BUTTER CUSTARD
Serves 4-5

INGREDIENTS
4-5 slices white bread
Butter
½ cup sultanas
3 eggs
2 cups milk
2 tablespoons sugar
1 teaspoon vanilla essence
Nutmeg

METHOD
Spread the bread with butter and either leave whole or cut into fingers.

Place sultanas in a greased ovenproof dish and cover with bread.

Beat eggs, milk, sugar and vanilla together and pour over bread. Allow to stand 20 minutes.

Sprinkle with nutmeg and bake in a moderate oven 35-40 minutes.

Serve warm with apple sauce.

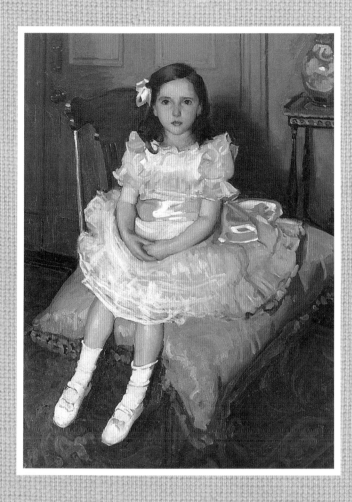

Hugh Ramsay
1877-1906
Portrait of Miss Nellie
Patterson c.1903
Oil on canvas 122.3 x 92.2cm
National Gallery of
Australia, Canberra

This little girl was born at
the end of the 19th century
into an affluent family as
the Australian colony
developed and prospered.
Her portrait was painted two
years after Federation,
presenting her in an
atmosphere of luxurious
comfort and as a pampered
and adored child dressed for
a party in ruffles and frills
with a satin sash. Perhaps it
was her own birthday party,
no doubt a lavish event with
an elaborate spread of
jellies, cakes, jam tarts and
home made lemonade.
Although she lived in a
faraway country, her life
would have been circum-
scribed by English town and
country manners and
customs, with nannies and
nursery teas, pony rides and
pets, an adopted rarified
lifestyle reserved only for a
special few settlers.

APRICOT RICE CREAM
Serves 5

INGREDIENTS
⅔ cup rice
2¾ cups milk
½ teaspoon vanilla
   essence
⅓ cup sugar
1 x 822g (26oz) can
   apricot halves
1 cup cream, whipped
1 egg white
Toasted almond slivers
Extra cream (optional)

METHOD
Pour 1 cup boiling water over rice, leave for 10 minutes and then drain.

Put rice into a saucepan, add milk and vanilla and cook gently, stirring occasionally, until rice is tender. Add sugar, stir until dissolved, put aside until cold.

Drain apricots, take out a third, chop into small pieces and fold into the rice, with the cream.

Beat egg white until stiff, fold in.

Turn into a serving bowl and chill. To serve, decorate with apricot halves, almond slivers and whipped cream.

Note: If you wish, omit cream from top and serve the sweet with apricot sauce. For the sauce, put ¾ cup canned apricot nectar into a saucepan, add 1 tablespoon brandy and heat. Mix 2 teaspoons arrowroot or cornflour to a paste with a little water, add to pan and stir until boiling. Add a pinch of cinnamon, serve when cold.

ICE CREAM ROMANOFF
Serves 2

INGREDIENTS
4 peach halves, sliced
12 strawberries
Vanilla ice-cream
Green peppermint
liqueur

METHOD
Arrange fruit in 2 parfait glasses. Top with ice-cream and pour over the liqueur.

SWEET RUM OMELETTE
Serves 4

INGREDIENTS
4 eggs, separated
4 tablespoons caster
  sugar
1 tablespoon butter

Sauce
(recipe follows)

METHOD
Preheat the griller to moderate. Beat egg yolks with 2 tablespoons of sugar until creamy.

Beat egg whites until stiff, gradually beat in rest of sugar and fold into the yolks.

Melt butter in a 20 cm (8 in) omelette pan, pour in mixture and cook over moderate heat 5-7 minutes, lifting side with spatula to test when underneath is golden.

Put omelette, in the pan, under the griller for a few minutes, or until top is firm and golden.

Fold in half, turn on to a warm serving dish, pour the sauce over and serve with vanilla ice-cream.

Sauce: Melt 125 g (4 oz) butter with 2 tablespoons caster sugar and grated rind of 1 medium-sized orange. When sugar has dissolved, add ¼ cup of rum, heat well, then set alight and pour over omelette.

ROLY POLY PUDDING
Serves 4-5

INGREDIENTS
1½ cups self-raising
  flour
125g (4oz) butter
1 tablespoon caster sugar
¼ cup mixture milk
  and water
½ cup loosely packed
  brown sugar
1 teaspoon ground
  ginger
½ teaspoon mixed spice
½ cup sultanas
½ cup currants
¼ cup chopped mixed
  peel

METHOD
Sift flour, rub in butter until mixture resembles fine breadcrumbs, mix in caster sugar.

Stir in enough of the milk and water to form a firm dough.

Knead lightly on a floured surface until smooth, roll out thinly to a rectangle. Mix together brown sugar and spices, sprinkle over pastry to 2.5 cm (1 in) from edges.

Sprinkle the sultanas, currants and peel over, brush edges with milk. Roll up as for a Swiss roll from the long edge, seal ends.

Lift on to a greased oven tray, brush over with milk and sprinkle with sugar. Bake in a moderately hot oven 25-30 minutes, or until golden brown.

CRÈME CARAMEL
Serves 6

INGREDIENTS
1 cup caster sugar
½ cup water
1½ cups milk
½ cup cream
⅓ cup sugar
4 eggs, beaten
1 teaspoon vanilla
  essence

METHOD
Place caster sugar and water in a small saucepan and stir over a low heat until sugar dissolves. Cook without stirring until golden brown and remove from heat immediately.

Take care not to burn.

Pour quickly into 6 individual greased moulds and rotate to coat the sides.

Heat milk and cream together. Add the ⅓ cup sugar and stir until dissolved. Cool to lukewarm. Pour onto beaten eggs and vanilla and mix well.

Pour into caramel lined moulds and place in a baking tin half filled with warm water.

Bake in a moderate oven 20–25 minutes until set. Remove from water and allow to cool.

Chill in refrigerator overnight. Run a knife carefully around sides if unmoulding, otherwise serve straight from dishes.

DUCHESS OF YORK PUDDING
Serves 4

INGREDIENTS
60g (2oz) butter
¼ cup sugar
2 eggs
1 cup self raising flour
2 tablespoons raspberry
  jam or marmalade
½ teaspoon bicarbonate
  of soda

METHOD
Beat butter and sugar until soft and creamy. Beat in eggs. Mix in flour, jam and bicarbonate of soda. Place in a greased pudding basin and cover with buttered paper.

Tie securely, place in a saucepan half filled with boiling water and allow to cook gently 1½ hours. Serve hot with custard.

Opposite page: Creme Caramel, recipe above.

ORANGE CRÉPES
Serves 8-9

INGREDIENTS

Crépes:
1 cup plain flour
Pinch salt
1 egg
1¼ cups milk
1 tablespoon butter,
 melted

Filling:
250g (8oz) packaged
 cream cheese
3 tablespoons sour cream
Grated rind 1 orange

Sauce:
60g (2oz) butter
¼ cup orange juice
3 tablespoons icing
 sugar
Grated rind 1 lemon
1 tablespoon lemon
 juice
½ cup orange brandy
 liqueur
½ cup brandy

METHOD

Sift flour and salt into a basin. Add egg and gradually stir in milk, beating until smooth. Stir in melted butter.

Heat a crépe pan, brush with melted butter, pour in ¼ cup batter, tilt pan to cover base completely and cook quickly on both sides. Repeat until all the batter is used.

Beat cream cheese, sour cream and orange rind together until creamy and spread on each crépe. Fold into 4 and place close together in a chafing dish.

Melt butter, stir in orange juice, icing sugar, lemon rind and juice and stir well. Add liqueur and heat thoroughly. Pour over crépes and re-heat, spooning sauce over crépes all the time.

Pour over warmed brandy and shake gently to spread it over crépes.

Ignite and serve flaming.

*Left: Orange Crepes,
recipe above.*

cup caster sugar 11/2 tablespoons butter 21/2 tablespoons cocoa 4 tal

ream filling: 1 cup cream 1 tablespoon cocoa, sifted 1 tablespoon cas

fted 1 tablespoon water Few drops of vanilla essence method Beat the

ntinue beating for about 15 minutes or until very thick and creamy.

ld into the egg mixture. Sift the flour and salt twice, sift again over

in) sandwich tins and bake in a moderate oven for 20-25 minutes, or

e fingertip and the cakes are beginning to shrink from the sides of th

til cold. Split each layer of cake in half. Join the layers together with

e surface with a spatula dipped in very hot water. Decorate with wa

Cakes, Pies and Breads

ns boiling water 11/4 cups self-raising flour Pinch of salt Walnut halv
ar Chocolate glacé icing: 1 cup icing sugar, sifted 2 tablespoons coco
ntil the yolks and whites are combined. Gradually beat in the sugar ar
e butter and cocoa to the boiling water, stir until combined, and the
ture, and fold in lightly and evenly. Divide between two greased 20 c
e tops of the cakes spring back immediately when touched lightly wit
Invert the cakes carefully on to a wire rack, remove the tins, and leav
am filling. Pour the glacé icing over immediately. If necessary, smoot
lves. Cream filling: Put the cream in a bowl and sprinkle the cocoa ar

APPLE-MARMALADE PIE
Serves 8

INGREDIENTS
1½ cups flour
Pinch salt
155g (5oz) butter
2 tablespoons hot water
1kg (2lb) Granny
   Smith apples, peeled
   and sliced
3 tablespoons
   marmalade
2-3 cloves
½ cup caster sugar
Unbeaten egg white
Extra sugar
Ground cinnamon

METHOD
Sift flour and salt, add the butter melted in the hot water and blend, adding flour or more hot water until mixture is a workable consistency. Roll out lightly on a floured board and line a 23 cm (9 in) springform cake tin.

Mix together the sliced apples, marmalade, cloves and sugar and place in the pastry case.

Brush edges with hot water and cover with remaining pastry, pressing edges together to seal. Decorate with pastry trimmings and make a vent in the centre for steam to escape.

Brush with unbeaten egg white, sprinkle generously with sugar and bake in a moderately hot oven 40-50 minutes until pastry is golden brown. Cover with foil if pastry is browning too much.

When ready to serve, dust with cinnamon. Serve hot or cold with whipped sweetened cream flavoured with cinnamon.

GEM SCONES
Makes 12-16

INGREDIENTS
1½ tablespoons softened
   butter
2 tablespoons sugar
1 egg
½ cup milk
1 cup self-raising flour
Pinch of salt

METHOD
Beat the butter with the sugar until creamy. Add the egg and beat well. Stir in the milk.

Sift together the flour and salt and fold in. Spoon into very hot, greased gem irons, filling to ¾. Bake in a hot oven for 10-15 minutes.

Opposite page:
Apple-Marmalade Pie.

LITTLE LEMON TARTS
Makes 20

INGREDIENTS
1¼ cups plain flour
½ teaspoon salt
2 tablespoons caster
   sugar
125g (4oz) butter
1 egg yolk
1 tablespoon lemon
   juice

Lemon Butter:
125g (4oz) butter
1 cup sugar
Finely grated rind of
   3 medium lemons
½ cup lemon juice
4 eggs, lightly beaten

METHOD
Sift dry ingredients together. Add the butter and rub in until the mixture resembles fine bread crumbs. Mix the egg yolk with the lemon juice and add to the flour. Mix together and knead gently to form a smooth ball. Wrap and chill for 30 minutes. Roll out on a floured surface and cut in circles to line fluted tartlet tins. Bake in a moderate oven 12-15 minutes or until light golden. Remove from tins and leave until cold. Fill with lemon butter. Serve with whipped cream.
Lemon butter: Melt the butter over hot water. Add the sugar and stir until dissolved. Mix in the lemon rind and juice. Quickly stir in the eggs. Stir over boiling water until mixture is thick enough to coat the back of a wooden spoon - about 5 minutes. Strain, pour into hot sterilised jars, and seal. When cold store in the refrigerator until needed.

PRESERVED LEMONS

INGREDIENTS
12 fresh lemons
Boiling water
Sugar

METHOD
Place lemons in a large saucepan and pour over boiling water to just cover. Cook gently until almost tender. Remove with a slotted spoon.

Measure liquid and add 2 cups sugar to 1½ cups liquid. Boil these two ingredients together for 5 minutes. Pierce lemons with a skewer, add to syrup and cook until softened. Place in wide-necked jars, cover with syrup, seal and leave 2 weeks before using.

Delicious served chilled and sliced with ice-cream for an unusual dessert.

Opposite page:
Sydney's north-west was the first area producing citrus fruits. Oranges and lemons were popular and used for delicacies such as Little Lemon Tarts, as well as Preserved Lemons, recipes above and Lemon Syrup, recipe page 93.

CINNAMON TEA CAKE

INGREDIENTS

1 cup self-raising flour
½ teaspoon cinnamon
¼ teaspoon nutmeg
1 egg, separated
½ cup sugar
½ cup milk
Vanilla essence
1½ tablespoons butter,
   melted
Extra melted butter
1 teaspoon cinnamon
1 tablespoon sugar

METHOD

Sift the flour with the ½ teaspoon of cinnamon and the nutmeg. Beat the egg white until stiff. Add the egg yolk and mix in. Gradually beat in the ½ cup of sugar. Slowly stir in the milk and vanilla essence. Stir in the sifted dry ingredients, with the melted butter.

   Spoon into a greased 18 cm (7 in) round sandwich tin and bake in a moderate oven for 30 minutes. While still hot, brush the top with extra melted butter and sprinkle with the teaspoon of cinnamon mixed with the tablespoon of sugar.

   Serve warm or cold, with butter.

CHEESE STRAWS
Makes 70

INGREDIENTS

½ cup plain flour
½ cup self-raising flour
½ teaspoon salt
¼ teaspoon paprika
Pinch of cayenne pepper
1½ cups grated matured
   Cheddar cheese
1 egg
¼ cup beer
Extra beer
Sesame seeds or coarse
   salt

METHOD

Sift the flours into a mixing bowl with the salt, paprika, and cayenne pepper. Stir in the cheese. Beat the egg lightly and stir in the beer. Pour over the flour and mix to a firm dough.

   Knead lightly on a floured surface, then roll out thinly and cut into 10 x 1 cm (4 x 1/2 in) strips. Arrange on an ungreased oven tray, brush lightly with beer, and sprinkle with sesame seeds or salt. Bake in a moderate oven for 15-20 minutes.

LAYERED CHOCOLATE SPONGE

INGREDIENTS

4 eggs
1 cup caster sugar
1½ tablespoons butter
2½ tablespoons cocoa
4 tablespoons boiling
 water
1¼ cups self-raising
 flour
Pinch of salt
Walnut halves

Cream filling:
1 cup cream
1 tablespoon cocoa,
 sifted
1 tablespoon caster
 sugar

Chocolate glacé icing:
1 cup icing sugar, sifted
2 tablespoons cocoa,
 sifted
1 tablespoon water
Few drops of vanilla
 essence

METHOD

Beat the eggs until the yolks and whites are combined.
Gradually beat in the sugar and continue beating for about
15 minutes or until very thick and creamy. Add the butter
and cocoa to the boiling water, stir until combined, and
then fold into the egg mixture.

Sift the flour and salt twice, sift again over the mixture,
and fold in lightly and evenly. Divide between two greased
20 cm (8 in) sandwich tins and bake in a moderate oven for
20-25 minutes, or until the tops of the cakes spring back
immediately when touched lightly with the fingertip and
the cakes are beginning to shrink from the sides of the tins.

Invert the cakes carefully on to a wire rack, remove the
tins, and leave until cold. Split each layer of cake in half.
Join the layers together with the cream filling. Pour the
glacé icing over immediately. If necessary, smooth the
surface with a spatula dipped in very hot water. Decorate
with walnut halves.

Cream filling: Put the cream in a bowl and sprinkle the
cocoa and sugar over. Chill for at least 30 minutes.
Whip until thick.

Chocolate glacé icing: Sift the icing sugar and cocoa
together and put in a saucepan with the water and vanilla
essence. Heat very carefully, stirring, until the mixture is of a
pouring consistency.

LEMON SYRUP

INGREDIENTS

3½ cups freshly
 squeezed lemon juice
4 cups sugar
2 teaspoons citric acid
2 teaspoons tartaric acid
2 teaspoons epsom salts

METHOD

Strain juice into a glass or china basin. Add all other
ingredients and stir until sugar is dissolved. Bottle and seal.

To serve, pour a small amount into a tall glass. Top with
chilled water or lemonade and add ice.

*Following pages:
Many of the new arrivals
who came from Britain
and Europe to populate
Australia brought their
favourite family "receipts"
with them. These recipes
have been absorbed into
our gastronomic culture.
One of the most popular
from Scotland was the
sweet crumbly buttery
biscuit-like cake called
shortbread, recipe above,
which is traditionally cut
or broken into segments
at the table.*

THE CROWN PRINCESS VICTORIA'S BIRTHDAY CAKE

INGREDIENTS

Walnut layer
1¼ cups walnut pieces
¼ cup icing sugar, sifted
2 egg whites

Meringue layer
2 egg whites
½ cup caster sugar
1½ cups cream, whipped
250g (8oz) fresh
  raspberries
Fondant or marzipan
  roses for decoration

METHOD

Grind walnuts in a food processor. Stir in icing sugar and mix to a paste with the unbeaten egg whites. Spread out into 2 x 20 cm (8 in) rounds on greased greaseproof paper on baking trays.

Bake in a moderate oven 10 minutes until firm to touch. Turn out onto wire racks and carefully peel off the paper. Cool.

Make meringue by beating the 2 egg whites until stiff. Add sugar gradually, beating all the time until thick. Spread out to a 20 cm (8 in) round on greased paper on a baking tray. Bake in a slow oven until dry and crisp, about 45-50 minutes. Cool and carefully remove paper.

Join the cake together on a serving plate by placing the meringue layer in the centre with whipped cream and raspberries between each layer. Completely cover with whipped cream and mould some roses from softened fondant or a marzipan roll. Colour pink with food colouring. Chill well before cutting.

SOMERSET SEED CAKE

INGREDIENTS

185g (6oz) butter
¾ cup caster sugar
2 teaspoons caraway seeds
3 eggs, separated
1 tablespoon ground
  almonds
2 cups self-raising flour
2 tablespoons milk
Extra caraway seeds

METHOD

Beat together butter and sugar until creamy, stir in the seeds. Beat egg whites until fairly stiff, add yolks and whisk in lightly, fold into the creamed mixture, with the almonds.

Sift the flour and fold in, with the milk. Turn into a large loaf tin, greased and lined on base with greased, greaseproof paper, top with a light sprinkling of caraway seeds. Bake in a moderate oven about 1 hour, or until done when tested. Leave in tin for 10 minutes, then turn out.

EDINBURGH SHORTBREAD

INGREDIENTS
250g (8oz) butter
½ cup caster sugar
2¼ cups plain flour
½ cup rice flour

METHOD
Cream butter and sugar. Gradually add flour and work with hands into a smooth creamy ball.

Press out on baking paper lined oven trays to form 2 x 20 cm (8 in) rounds, 1 cm (½ in) thick. Pinch a frill around the edge and mark lightly into 8 wedges. Pierce all over with a fork.

Bake in a moderately slow oven 20 minutes until a pale straw colour. Cool slightly then cut through the marked lines.

PRESTON GINGERBREAD

INGREDIENTS
2 cups plain flour
¼ teaspoon nutmeg
2 teaspoons ground
   ginger
⅓ cup brown sugar
125g (4oz) butter
⅓ cup golden syrup
⅓ cup treacle
1 teaspoon bicarbonate
   of soda
1¼ cups warm milk
1 egg, lightly beaten
Slivered blanched
   almonds

METHOD
Sift together flour and spices, stir in the sugar. Put butter, syrup and treacle into a saucepan and gently heat until butter has melted. Stir bicarbonate of soda into the warm milk.

Add butter mixture and milk to dry ingredients, with the egg, stir in to combine well. Pour into a 28 x 18 cm (11 x 7 in) lamington tin, greased and lined on base with baking paper.

Sprinkle almonds over and bake in a moderately slow oven about 1 hour.

Following pages: Bush damper, recipe page 100 Bush Damper, was a rough bush bread of flour and water without leavening, baked on the bush campfire coals. It was part of the original staple diet of the Australian settlers. They sometimes ate it with a slab of fried dried meat, sometimes spread with; golden syrup, "bullocky's joy", always with billy tea and maybe a swig of rum.

BUSH DAMPER

INGREDIENTS

3 cups self-raising flour
2 teaspoons salt
3 tablespoons butter
½ cup milk
½ cup water

METHOD

Sift flour and salt into a bowl, rub in butter until mixture resembles fine crumbs.

Make a well in the centre, add the combined milk and water, mix lightly with a knife until dough leaves sides of bowl.

Gently knead on a lightly floured surface and then knead into a round, put on a greased oven tray. Pat into a round 15-16 cm (6-6½ in) diameter.

Bake in a hot oven for 10 minutes, or until golden brown. Reduce heat to moderate and bake another 20 minutes. Eat the day it is made. For variation, add ¾ cup grated Cheddar cheese.

POTATO SCONES
Makes 8

INGREDIENTS

250g (8oz) dry
    mashed potato
1 tablespoon butter
Pinch salt and pepper
¼ – ½ cup plain flour

METHOD

Place mashed potato into a basin and mix in butter, salt and pepper. Add flour gradually, adding just enough to mix into a soft, dry consistency.

Knead on a lightly floured board. Roll out thinly and cut into 8 squares or rounds.

Pierce well all over with a fork.

Cook on a greased hot griddle or frying pan 2-3 minutes. Turn when brown and cook on other side. May be served hot or cold. May be spread with butter and are delicious served with bacon.

Desiderious Orban
Morning 1959
Pastel on paper 56 x 76cm
Bathurst Regional Art Gallery

APPLE STRAWBERRY TART
Serves 6

INGREDIENTS
2 cups plain flour
155g (5oz) butter
2 tablespoons sugar
2 tablespoons cold
  water
3-4 cooking apples
½ cup strawberry
  conserve
1 egg, beaten, for glaze

METHOD
Place flour in a basin and rub in butter with fingertips. Stir in sugar.

Add water and mix into a dough. Chill.

Roll out two-thirds of the pastry and line a 23 cm (9 in) pie plate. Peel, core and slice apples into pastry case. Spread strawberry conserve over the top. Roll remaining pastry and cut into strips. Brush with egg and place in a lattice design over top and place another strip around the edge. Brush pastry again with beaten egg.

Bake in a hot oven 30 minutes until browned and cooked. Serve warm with whipped cream or ice-cream.

JAM PASTRIES
Makes about 30

INGREDIENTS
90g (3oz) butter
2 tablespoons sugar
1 teaspoon grated
lemon rind
1 egg
1¼ cups plain flour
Thick raspberry jam
1 egg, beaten, for glaze
Coarse sugar

METHOD
Beat butter, sugar and lemon rind together until creamy. Beat in egg. Add flour and work into a dough. Chill thoroughly until firm enough for easy handling.

Roll out on a lightly floured surface and cut with a fluted cutter, about 8 cm (3 in). Place on greased baking trays, place a small amount of jam in the centre and fold in halves.

Brush tops with beaten egg and sprinkle with sugar. Bake in a moderate oven until cooked and lightly brown, about 15 minutes. Cool.

Opposite page: Apple Strawberry Tart

OAT WAFERS
Makes about 24

INGREDIENTS
1¼ cups rolled oats
90g (3oz) butter,
    melted
1 egg
¾ cup sugar
2 tablespoons self-raising
    flour

METHOD
Place oats in a bowl, pour over melted butter and allow to stand 10 minutes to soften oats slightly. Mix in egg, sugar and flour.

Place small portions well apart onto greased baking trays to allow room for spreading. Flatten out with the back of a spoon. Bake in a moderate oven 10 minutes until cooked and brown.

Allow to cool for a few minutes before removing carefully with a spatula. These delicious biscuits become crisp when cool and are worth the careful handling when removing from oven trays.

COFFEE BUTTER CAKE

INGREDIENTS
1¼ cups self-raising
    flour
¾ cup lightly filled
    brown sugar
2 teaspoons instant
    coffee
90g (3oz) butter,
    melted
2 eggs
3 tablespoons cream
1 x 100g block
    chocolate
Blanched almonds

METHOD
Place flour, sugar and instant coffee in a bowl. Stir in melted butter, eggs and cream and beat until smooth.

Pour into a greased 5-cup loaf tin and bake in a moderate oven 35–40 minutes until cooked. Cool.

Melt chocolate gently, spread over top of cake and decorate with almonds.

Opposite page:
Clockwise from right:
Coffee Butter Cake,
recipe page 104, Jam
Pasrties, recipe page 108,
and Pat Wafers, recipe
above.

Margaret Preston
1875-1963
Still Life 1926
Oil on canvas 50.8 x 56cm
Bequest of Adrian Feint 1972
Art Gallery of New South Wales

WELSH RAREBIT
Serves 4

INGREDIENTS
60g (2oz) butter

1 teaspoon prepared English mustard

½ teaspoon salt

Freshly ground pepper

1 egg yolk, beaten

1 teaspoon Worcestershire sauce

125g (4oz) tasty cheese, grated

3 tablespoons beer (flat beer will do)

4 slices hot, buttered toast

METHOD
Melt the butter in a saucepan over low heat, and stir in mustard, salt and pepper to taste. Stir in egg yolk, sauce and cheese. Continue stirring until cheese melts, then stir in beer and heat through.

(Do not allow to boil.)

Taste for seasoning, and serve at once over hot buttered toast. For lunch, you might like to add pickled onions and a green salad.

NOTE: If you wish, the rarebit can be browned quickly under a hot grill after it is spread on toast.

WELSH SPECKLED BREAD (BARA BRITH)
Makes 2 loaves

INGREDIENTS
90g (3oz) butter

4 cups plain flour

½ cup brown sugar

1 cup sultanas

1 cup currants

½ cup raisins

⅓ cup chopped mixed peel

¼ teaspoon salt

½ teaspoon mixed spice

1 cup milk

1 x 7g sachet dry yeast or 15g (½oz) compressed yeast

1 egg, beaten

METHOD
Rub butter into flour with fingertips. Stir in sugar, fruits, peel, salt and spice and make a well in the centre.

Heat milk to lukewarm and pour a little into yeast and stir until melted. Add egg yeast and remaining milk to basin and mix into a soft dough. Place in a greased bowl, cover with plastic wrap and leave in a warm place until doubled in volume, about 1 hour.

Knead thoroughly on a lightly floured surface and divide in half. Place in 2 greased 6-cup loaf tins, cover with plastic wrap and allow to stand in a warm place 30-40 minutes. Bake in a moderately hot oven 30 minutes, reduce heat to moderately slow, cover tops lightly with foil if browning too much and bake another 15-20 minutes, until cooked. This delicious Welsh teabread is served thinly sliced with butter.

Following pages:
Welsh Rarebit and Welsh Speckled Bread (Bara Brith), recipes above.

IRISH SODA BREAD
Serves 4

INGREDIENTS
1 tablespoon butter
1 cup self raising flour
2 cups plain flour
1 teaspoon salt
1 teaspoon bicarbonate
  of soda
1 cup cooked, sieved
  potato
1 egg
1¼ cups buttermilk

METHOD
Rub butter into sifted dry ingredients. Mix in potato. Mix in egg beaten with half the buttermilk and gradually stir in enough remaining buttermilk to form a soft dough.

Place in a greased 20 cm (8 in) sandwich cake tin, cut a cross in the top with a sharp knife and bake in a moderately hot oven 35 minutes until cooked.

For a soft crust, brush while hot with melted butter.

WINDSOR CAKE
Serves 10-12

INGREDIENTS
250g (8oz) butter
1½ cups sugar
4 eggs
1 cup milk
4 cups self raising flour

METHOD
Beat butter and sugar until soft and creamy. Beat in eggs one at a time.

Add milk and sifted flour and beat until smooth.

Place in a greased deep 20 cm (8 in) cake tin and bake in a moderate oven until cooked, about 1¼ hours. Keeps well.

CHEESE DAMPER

INGREDIENTS
2 cups self-raising flour
½ teaspoon of salt
1 cup of milk
1½ tablespoons softened
  margarine
¾ cup grated Cheddar
  cheese

METHOD
Sift the flour and salt together. Add the milk, butter, and cheese. Beat for 1 to 2 minutes with a wooden spoon. Pour into a greased and floured 18-centimetre (7- inch) sandwich tin and bake in a hot oven for 25-30 minutes. Serve sliced with butter.

ECCLES CAKES
Makes 8

INGREDIENTS
125g (4oz) butter
2 cups plain flour
3-4 tablespoons cold
   water
1½ cups currants
½ cup finely chopped
   mixed peel
¼ cup sugar
½ teaspoon nutmeg
2 tablespoons butter
1 egg white, beaten
   lightly
Caster sugar

METHOD
Rub the 125 g (4 oz) butter into flour and add enough
cold water to mix into a firm dough. Chill. Place currants,
mixed peel, sugar, nutmeg and the 2 tablespoons butter
into a saucepan and stir over a low heat until butter melts.
Pour into a basin and allow to cool.

Roll out pastry and cut into 8 rounds, using a saucer.
Divide fruit mixture between the circles, gather up edges
and pinch together. Turn over, roll lightly and brush with
the egg white. Sprinkle with caster sugar and make 3 small
slits in the top.

Place on greased baking trays and bake in a hot oven
15-20 minutes until lightly browned.

APPLE SPONGE
Serves 4-5

INGREDIENTS
1 cup self raising flour
Pinch salt
½ cup caster sugar
1 egg
90g (3oz) butter,
   melted
4 cooking apples, peeled
   and sliced

METHOD
Place flour, salt and sugar in a basin. Beat in egg and melted
butter.

Place apples in a greased shallow 5-cup ovenproof dish.

Spoon cake mixture over apples and bake in a moderate
oven 45-50 minutes until cooked.

Serve warm with whipped cream or custard.

CHEESE FLAN
Serves 6-8

INGREDIENTS
125g (4oz) butter
2 cups plain flour
3 tablespoons cold
   water
125g (4oz) tasty
   cheese, cut into small
   cubes
125g (4oz) Swiss
   cheese, cut into small
   cubes
1 small onion, grated
4 eggs
¾ cup cream
½ cup sour cream
2 tablespoons grated
Parmesan cheese
½ teaspoon paprika
Salt and pepper

METHOD
Make pastry by rubbing butter into the flour and mix into
a dough with the water. Chill 1 hour. Press evenly over
base and sides of a fluted 28 cm (11 in) flan tin with
removable base.

Pierce well with a fork and bake in a hot oven 10
minutes.

Combine tasty cheese, Swiss cheese and grated onion.
Place evenly over base of pastry.

Beat eggs, cream, sour cream and Parmesan cheese
together. Season with paprika, salt and pepper to taste and
pour into pastry case.

Return to oven and bake a further 30-35 minutes until
cooked. If topping is browning too much, cover lightly with
a piece of foil. Serve freshly made with salad.

ORANGE BREAD

INGREDIENTS
1 tablespoon finely
   grated orange rind
60g (2oz) margarine
½ cup sugar
1 egg
1½ cups self-raising
   flour
½ cup milk
chopped mixed peel
extra sugar

METHOD
Work the orange rind into the margarine then gradually
beat in the sugar. Add the egg and beat in well. Sift the
flour and fold alternately with the milk. Turn into a greased
20 x 10 centimetre (8 x 4 in) loaf tin. Smooth the surface
and sprinkle lightly with the chopped mixed peel and extra
sugar. Bake in a moderately hot oven for about 35 minutes,
or until done when tested.

Opposite page:
Cheese Flan, recipe
above.

The Second Hundred Years

Margaret Preston
1875-1963
Implement Blue 1927
Oil on canvas on paperboard
42.5 x 43cm
Gift of the artist 1960
Art Gallery of New South Wales

The Second Hundred Years

Lamingtons, as all Australians know are simply squares of plain cake dipped in melted chocolate and sugar and coated in desiccated coconut. They are supposed to have been named after Baron Lamington, governor of Queensland from 1895 to 1901.

Peach Melba was created in 1894 by Escoffier in honour of the Australian singer Dame Nellie Melba. It consists of a fresh peach poached in vanilla-flavoured sugar syrup, peeled, set on a layer of icecream, coated with fresh raspberry purée and served in an individual or crystal dish.

These two confections, and damper, were probably the only culinary inventions which Australia could call her own at the turn-of the-century. Between Federation in 1901 and the end of the Great War in 1918, our food habits didn't change much, apart from the necessary wartime tightening of belts. Patriotic cookery books of the time popularised a few new recipes such as Anzac Biscuits and Soldier's Christmas Cake, which anxious wives and mothers lovingly baked and packed in food parcels to send to the trenches.

The average Australian takes no aesthetic pleasure in food scoffed the Melbourne playwright, Louis Esson in 1918. However, at the end of the 19th century, speculation, building and land development, had spawned visions of wealth and power which spilled over into the 20th. Prosperity had produced a fashion for grand balls, receptions and large public banquets to honour special events or people, such as the Grand Federation Dinner in January, 1901. These were outstanding affairs, not for average Australians, but for the elite, the officials and politicians. Menus were elaborate but uninspired, with a profusion of Anglo-French dishes, and an embarrassment of wines, especially French champagne. Here is a menu for one consular dinner celebrating Queen Victoria's birthday:

Salad Russe
Cressy Soup
Clear Soup
Whiting Timbale
Schnapper grilled á la Tartare

Entrée
Vol-au-vent of Spring Chicken
Sweetbread with Tomato Sauce
Roast Turkey

Removes
Grilled Ham
Fillet of Lamb with Olives
Charlotte of Apples
Pineapple Cream
Nessebrode Pudding
Findon Haddock on Toast
Cheese Fritter

Champagne luncheons featuring cold fowl and ham, as well as wines and beer, were a fashionable pursuit among the new moneyed society in this age of opulence. They were customary at public land sales, big auctions and race meetings. Picnics on a grand scale

were another. In 1868 when Prince Edward, Duke of Edinburgh, was visiting Australia, at a picnic in his honour in Sydney, guests ate fresh oysters, bread and butter and stout in the morning, lobster, chicken and champagne in the afternoon.

The boom in restaurants which had begun with the Gold Rush and popularised mixed grills and carpetbag steak, continued into the 20th century as the population increased. The first free settlers had begun arriving in the 1820s, full of vitality and optimism. They continued to pour in until the first government immigration schemes began and the country grew from a colony to a nation. The divisions of the classes were still strictly defined, but these working class people were the harbingers of the rising middle class which would eventually dominate the structure of our emerging society and its cuisine.

Dining at home depended on wealth and status. In the towns, for the very rich and well-to-do, it was elaborate and formal. For the working class it was simple, revolving around roast meat with gravy, baked potatoes and vegetables, and a pudding, for midday dinner every Sunday. On Monday, the meat was eaten cold, perhaps with shredded lettuce salad and homemade boiled mayonnaise. Thus, for the poor, dining was a monotonous, usually inadequate affair.

When a young married newspaperman, Joseph Elliott, wrote home to his mother in England describing his family life in their Adelaide cottage in the 1860s, he was simply reinforcing an established way of life perpetuated by ordinary people: *Well, after Church (on Sunday), we dine in our sitting room, and come when you will, you will always find the same dinner! We consume 52 legs of mutton a year! Baked in the oven and also a few baked potatoes. After that we have English jam tarts or something of the sort but generally the tarts are preferred, at all events six or seven months out of the twelve. After that we generally have a few apples or something of the sort. Monday. I get to town between 8 and 9, taking some lunch with me for 1 o'clock, leave town at about 5 and dine on cold mutton and warm potatoes with mint sauce, of which I am very fond. Tuesday. We generally dine on either mutton or beef; beef or mutton—not much change here.*[5]

In Sydney and Melbourne in the 20s, life was busy and colourful, with thriving markets and a multitude of busy pubs. The clip clop of the baker's carthorse or the rattle of milk bottles in the street at dawn were familiar sounds. Chinese vegetable men, rabbit and fish sellers and street market stalls were familiar sights as they had been since the 1850s when food vendors with old cries, tempted passers-by to pig's trotters, saveloys and bottled oysters. In Sydney, Charlie the Pieman carried his hot chicken, meat and cherry pies about in a basket. Little meat pies eaten hot with tomato sauce eventually became an Australian institution. With the linking of the railway lines and more opportunities for travel, they were nicknamed 'railway pies', and in some parts of the country eaten in bowls of thick pea soup and called 'floaters'.

Meanwhile, in the bush, life went on as it had since the opening up of rich pasture lands on the Bathurst Plains a hundred years before. It was a struggle for the 'cockatoo farmers' or 'cockles' as the smallholders were called, but a life of comparative ease for the 'silver tails', the bush aristocracy with their sprawling homesteads and enormous properties. They had mahogany furniture, polished cedar floors, fine china, silver and glass and kept house servants. These landowning families played a paternal role to their employees, the station hands, stockmen and shearers who ate meat three times a day and got drunk on Saturdays.

But in the wattle and daub huts of the poorest settlers, life was hard. They lived off the land, and women worked as hard as the men. They preserved their food by salting, drying, boiling in sugar syrup or fermenting. They cooked on open fires or camp ovens, made bread, butter, cheese and soap; dug potatoes, grew vegetables, dried their fruit, cured bacon and carried water. Their store rooms were filled with their own jams, pickles, chutneys, preserves, cordials, ginger beer and cough mixture. Despite loneliness, heat, dust, blowflies, bushfires and drought, the strongest survived.

For recreation there were bush dances, travelling circuses, church suppers, country shows and race meetings, weddings, christenings and funerals. In this

[5] *Our Home in Australia. A Description of Cottage Life in 1860 by Joseph Elliott. The Flannel Flower Press. Sydney, 1984.*

environment women cultivated their skills in baking and struggled to produce decent family meals. There were no ice chests or refrigeration, only Coolgardie safes and ingenuity. Jellies were made with isinglass. Blancmanges and trifles were wrapped in wet cloths and carried in their moulds by buggy to celebrations where the community shared their food.

From no ice to ice boxes to refrigerators; from wood stoves to gas to electricity; with advances in food technology and transport, and the introduction of canning and freezing, the old-fashioned Australian diet began to stir itself into the 20th century.

In many ways, 1929 was significant. It was the first year of the Depression which lasted into the mid-30s. Unemployment, dole queues, austerity meals and soup kitchens took much of the fun out of life, which the cinema replaced with celluloid dreams of romance and escape. 'Swaggies', itinerant unemployed men, wandered the country with their swags on their backs and only their dogs for company, looking for work outside the cities.

This was the year that Chef Herbert Sachse of the Hotel Esplanade in Perth, invented the pavlova, in honour of Anna Pavlova. It was a symphony of meringue, cream and passionfruit to celebrate the great Russian ballerina's visit.

In 1929 the first of the stream of persecuted Jews fleeing from the regimes of Hitler and Mussolini began to flow in. We called them 'refugees'. Many of them set up Polish-Austrian-German style delicatessens, butcher shops, bakeries and patisseries, stimulating our 'meat and potatoes' appetites with flavour sensations from their old traditional backgrounds.

When the Second World War broke out in 1939, the American troops who came to the Pacific intrigued us even more with their hamburgers, hot dogs, club sandwiches, milk shakes, Coca Cola, chicken Maryland, Boston baked beans and barbecues.

By 1947, with the fall of Singapore, an influx of Dutch civilians escaping from the Japanese added their Dutch-Indonesian dishes to our repertoire. Nasi goreng and rijsttafel joined the curries and other exotic dishes we had inherited earlier from the British Raj, such as kedgeree, and mulligatawny.

Post-war, immigration from Europe and the Mediterranean countries revolutionised our food habits forever. Italians, Greeks and new arrivals from all over the world introduced us to garlic, herbs, pasta, tomato paste, patés and terrines, and all the other delights of their culinary heritages.

Mrs Beeton was the food guru of the 19th century, and Elizabeth David was the leader of the new wave of cookery we fell in love with after the war. *Mediterranean Food*, her first cookery book, was published in England in 1950, and followed by others. They made a great impression on Australian women, and coincided with their burgeoning interest in food from other lands, as well as setting off the phenomenal 20th century avalanche of cookbooks, many of the best by Australians.

We have grown used to food cults and fads. We have learned that nutrition, good health, fitness and sensible eating can influence our life spans. Vegetarian cookery, health foods, macrobiotics, slimming diets, and *nouvelle cuisine* have contributed to our improved eating habits and food presentation. Proliferating restaurants, supermarkets, speciality food shops, caterers, takeaways, microwave ovens, electrical gadgets and convenience foods have simplified our lives. The impact of the working woman, with less time to spend on cooking, is still an unknown quantity. Food gurus on radio, television and in magazines and newspapers, colour food photography, professional *bon vivants* and consultants, cooking schools, and food advertising campaigns have intensified our interest in gastronomy.

Today our population has been stimulated by a huge proportion of people from other countries. We share a rich, fascinating assortment of culinary traditions and a bountiful supply of fresh food and produce. But the delicious hybrid dishes we set on our tables today are only a taste of a truly multinational style of cookery which will surely develop over the next 100 years and come to be known as Australian cuisine.

utmeg, Sour cream, Parsley, chopped, Croûtons, method; Peel, remov
nd salt. Pour in just enough water to cover and cook gently, with the
food processor with the milks (or push through a sieve and then sti
over and simmer for 5-7 minutes. Serve with a swirl of sour cream
eparately. 750g (1/2 lb) pumpkin, 1 medium onion, chopped, 1 teaspo
ream, Parsley, chopped, Croûtons, method; Peel, remove seeds from p
just enough water to cover and cook gently, with the lid on, until the
ith the milks (or push through a sieve and then stir in the milk). Retu
r 5-7 minutes. Serve with a swirl of sour cream and a sprinkling of
move seeds from pumpkin, and cut into pieces. Put into a saucepan

Soups

rom pumpkin, and cut into pieces. Put into a saucepan with the onio
ntil the pumpkin is tender. Purée the contents of the pan in a blende
nilk). Return the purée to the saucepan, adding the sugar and nutme
prinkling of parsley on each bowl and serve a bowl of crisp croûton
Water, 2 cups milk, 2 teaspoons sugar, Pinch of grated nutmeg, Sou
and cut into pieces. Put into a saucepan with the onion and salt. Pou
n is tender. Purée the contents of the pan in a blender or food processo
urée to the saucepan, adding the sugar and nutmeg. Cover and simme
on each bowl Sour cream, Parsley, chopped, Croûtons, method; Pee
onion and salt. Pour in just enough water

BORSCH
Serves 8

INGREDIENTS
1kg (2lb) shin of beef
8 cups water
1 onion, chopped
3 bay leaves
1 tablespoon whole
    allspice
2 teaspoons salt
2 tomatoes, peeled and
    chopped
2 potatoes, cut into thin
    strips
2 carrots, cut into thin
    strips
1 small cabbage,
    shredded
750g (1½lb)
    beetroot, cut into thin
    strips
2 teaspoons vinegar
Salt and freshly ground
    pepper
¼ cup chopped parsley
2 tablespoons snipped
    fresh dill

METHOD
Place beef, water, onion, bay leaves, allspice and salt into a
large saucepan and bring to boil. Skim if necessary and
cook with lid on for 1 hour or until tender.

While meat is cooking collect all the vegetables together.
It is best to be patient and use a sharp knife to cut the
vegetables (if they are grated the soup will be cloudy).

When meat is cooked remove from the pot. Cut into
thick strips from the bone and place meat back into the
pot. Add all the vegetables and allow to boil without the lid
for about 15 minutes. If you cook with the lid on, the soup
will not retain its bright attractive colour.

Stir in vinegar, salt, pepper, parsley and dill. Serve piping
hot with a spoonful of whipped cream flavoured with
horseradish cream and black bread.

Opposite page:
Borsch, recipe above.

CHILLED CUCUMBER YOGHURT SOUP
Serves 4

INGREDIENTS
1 medium-sized
  cucumber
1 teaspoon salt
1 large clove garlic
1 tablespoon wine
  vinegar
2 teaspoons finely
  chopped fresh dill
2 cups natural yoghurt
1 tablespoon chopped
  fresh mint

METHOD
Peel cucumber if necessary and slice thinly. Sprinkle with
the salt. Rub a bowl with the cut garlic clove and pour in
the vinegar, dill and yoghurt. Stir thoroughly.

Mix in the cucumber slices and sprinkle mint over
the top.

Chill for about 5 minutes in freezer and serve.

PROVENÇALE VEGETABLE SOUP
Serves 6-8

INGREDIENTS
6 cups water
1 cup diced potato
1 cup diced carrot
1 large leek, cut into
  strips
1 cup sliced green beans
Salt
1 x 310g can butter
  beans
½ cup broken pieces
  spaghetti
½ cup soft breadcrumbs
2 cloves garlic
2 tablespoons tomato
  paste
2 tablespoons fresh basil
  leaves
¼ cup grated Parmesan
  cheese
1 teaspoon curry paste
2 tablespoons olive oil

METHOD
Place water in a large saucepan, add potato, carrot, leek,
green beans and salt to taste.

Cook for 20 minutes with lid on. Add butter beans,
spaghetti and breadcrumbs and cook another 15-20 minutes
until spaghetti is tender.

Pulverise garlic, tomato paste, basil, Parmesan and curry
paste in a blender. Beat in olive oil a few drops at a time. If
desired may be worked to a paste with a pestle and mortar.

Stir into hot soup and serve.

CHILLED AVOCADO SOUP

Serves 4

INGREDIENTS

2 large ripe avocados,
 peeled and stoned
3 cups strong chicken
 stock
2 teaspoons lemon juice
Salt and freshly ground
 pepper
½ cup cream
Extra cream, whipped
Watercress

METHOD

Purée avocados in a blender with chicken stock and lemon juice.

Stir in salt, pepper and cream. Chill thoroughly.

Serve in bowls, topped with a little whipped cream and chopped watercress.

GREEK CHICKEN SOUP

Serves 6-8

INGREDIENTS

1 x 1kg (2lb) chicken
6 cups water
1 carrot sliced
1 onion sliced
1 stalk celery, sliced
1 teaspoon fresh thyme
1 bay leaf
2 garlic cloves, chopped
Salt to taste
2 teaspoons whole
 white peppercorns
¼ cup rice
1 tablespoon vegetable
 oil
1 egg yolk
2 eggs
Juice 1 lemon
Snipped chives

METHOD

Place chicken, water, carrot, onion, celery, thyme, bay leaf, garlic, salt and peppercorns in a large saucepan. Bring to boil, skim if necessary and cook until chicken is tender.

Remove chicken from stock and allow to cool. Cut into small pieces.

Strain stock and chill. Remove fat from top of stock. Sauté rice in the hot oil for a few minutes, add to the chicken stock and cook 15-18 minutes until rice is cooked. Stir in chicken. Taste for seasoning and add more salt and pepper if necessary. If a more filling soup is desired, double the amount of rice.

Beat egg yolk, eggs and lemon juice together and carefully beat in to this a little of the hot soup. Add. this to the rest of the hot soup, stirring all the time. Do not allow to boil, only re-heat, otherwise the soup will curdle. Serve immediately with bread and cheese.

Sprinkle snipped chives over top.

Following pages:
Clockwise from top right:
Provençale Vegetable
Soup, recipe page 126;
Seafood Soup, recipe page
130; Greek Chicken
Soup, recipe above.

CREAMY PRAWN SOUP
Serves 4

INGREDIENTS
1kg (2lb) prawns
1 onion, chopped
1 cup chopped celery
 (include green tops)
4 cups water
2 tablespoons butter
2 tablespoons flour
Salt and pepper
1 tablespoon tomato
 paste
½ cup dry white wine
½ cup cream

METHOD
Shell prawns and reserve a few for garnish. Place the remainder in a food processor and purée.

Place prawn shells, onion and celery in the water and bring to boil. Cook 20 minutes and then allow to cool. Strain.

Melt butter, add flour, salt and pepper to taste and stir 2-3 minutes over a low heat.

Add prawn liquid and stir until thickened and boiling. Stir in tomato paste and wine and cook gently 10 minutes.

Stir in puréed prawns and cream and heat through gently. Do not allow to boil because this may cause the soup to curdle. Place in warmed soup bowls and garnish with whipped cream, the reserved prawns and fine strips of lemon rind.

SEAFOOD SOUP
Serves 4-6

INGREDIENTS
1 leek
1 fennel bulb
½ cup sliced celery
8 mushrooms, sliced
1 clove garlic, crushed
3 tablespoons olive oil
4 cups fish stock
1 bay leaf
2 teaspoons lemon juice
Salt and pepper
500g (1lb) gemfish, diced
125g (4oz) scallops
4-6 scampi or king
 prawns, shelled
¼ cup dry white wine
½ cup whole egg
 mayonnaise
3 cloves garlic, crushed
Croûtons

METHOD
Wash leek and cut into strips together with the fennel bulb.

Add celery, mushrooms, garlic and cook in the hot oil for 10 minutes. Stir in fish stock, bay leaf, lemon juice, salt and pepper to taste. Simmer 5 minutes.

Add diced fish and scallops and cook gently 5 minutes. Stir in scampi or king prawns, wine and taste to see if more seasoning is needed. Re-heat gently.

Mix mayonnaise and garlic together, if too thick stir in some cream. Serve soup in bowls with croûtons and spoon on a little of the mayonnaise mixture.

Opposite page:
Creamy Prawn Soup,
recipe above.

Margaret Preston
1875-1963
Thea Proctor's Tea Party 1924
Oil on canvas 55.9 x 45.7cm
purchased 1942
Art Gallery of New South Wales

TUNA CHOWDER
Serves 4-6

INGREDIENTS
250g (8oz) potatoes,
    peeled and diced
1 tablespoon butter
2 bacon rashers, cut into
    small squares, with
    rind removed
2 medium onions, thinly
    sliced
1 x 375ml can
    evaporated milk
Salt and pepper
1 x 425g can tuna
Chopped parsley

METHOD
Cook the potatoes in 2 cups of boiling salted water for
about 8 minutes; remove the pan from the heat. Melt the
butter and gently fry the bacon and onions until the onions
are transparent and the bacon is crisp; drain and add to the
potatoes in the saucepan. Gradually stir in the evaporated
milk, then season with salt and pepper. Simmer for 10
minutes. Drain and flake the tuna, add to pan, and simmer
for 5-7 minutes, or until heated through.

Sprinkle with chopped parsley.

CHICKEN NOODLE SOUP
Serves 4-6

INGREDIENTS
1 cooked boiling fowl
    (see recipe Settler's
    Chicken, page 40)
250g (8oz) noodles
4 cups chicken stock
    (see recipe Settler's
    Chicken, page 40)
Salt and pepper
¼ cup chopped parsley

METHOD
Remove chicken skin and bones and cut flesh into
bite-sized pieces. Cook noodles in boiling salted water until
almost tender. Drain and add to hot chicken stock with
chicken pieces. Taste for seasoning.

Bring slowly to boil and simmer. Serve hot.

gredients 500 g (1lb) firm-fleshed fish fillets 13/4 cups water 1 small c
(4oz) scallops, split into halves 185 g (6oz) small mushrooms, thinly s
og (8oz) prawns, shelled and deveined Buttered breadcrumbs method
eat the water with the celery, onion, parsley, bay leaf, and wine u
emove the fish with a slotted spoon and put aside. Add the scallops t
easure and reserve 11/4 cups. Cook the mushrooms and shallots gent
aped individual ovenproof dishes, or into a shallow ovenproof dish
e reserved fish stock and cook, stirring until boiling. Simmer for 3-4
3 minutes to reheat. Spoon into the dishes or dish. Top with butter
edium heat until crisp). Put into a hot oven to reheat. Remove the fi

Seafood

lk 1/2 small onion 2 parsley sprigs 1 bay leaf 2/3 cup dry white wine 1:
nallots, finely chopped Butter Salt and pepper 1 tablespoon plain flou
skin from the fish and cut the flesh into small cubes, taking out bone
ng. Simmer for 5 minutes. Add the fish and simmer until just tende
n and simmer for 5 minutes. Remove the scallops and strain the liqui
ter until softened. Add salt and pepper to taste. Spoon into 4-6 she
ablespoon butter, add the flour, and stir for a minute. Gradually ac
. Add salt and pepper, then the fish, prawns, and scallops. Simmer f
s (about 6 tablespoons tossed in 3 tablespoons of melted butter ov
slotted spoon and put aside. Add the scallops to the pan and simm

SMOKED SALMON APPETISERS
Serves 4

INGREDIENTS
4 bread slices, buttered
4 smoked salmon slices
½ cup whipped cream
1 teaspoon horseradish
  cream
250g (8oz) prawns,
  shelled

METHOD
Fry bread on both sides until crisp and brown. Place on small serving plates and cover with smoked salmon.

Mix cream and horseradish together, spoon onto salmon and top with prawns.

Garnish with a sprig of fresh dill.

CREAMED MUSSELS
Serves 6 entrées

INGREDIENTS
36 fresh mussels
Water to cover
60g (2oz) butter
2 tablespoons plain
  flour
1½ cups cooking liquid
  from mussels
1 clove garlic, crushed
⅓ cup dry white wine
2 egg yolks
2 tablespoons lemon
  juice
⅓ cup cream
Salt and freshly ground
  pepper
Finely chopped parsley
  to garnish

METHOD
Wash mussels in cold, running water and scrub with a stiff brush until clean. Discard any that are not tightly closed. Place in a wide saucepan, cover with boiling water, and boil rapidly for 5 minutes, or until they open. Discard any that do not open.

Remove mussels from their shells, reserving the best shells for serving the mussels.

Strain the cooking liquid and save 1⅓ cups.

Melt the butter, stir in flour over low heat, and cook for 1 minute. Remove from heat and stir in the warm cooking liquid and the garlic. Bring to the boil and simmer for 5 minutes. Whisk wine, egg yolks, lemon juice and cream together and stir into pan. Continue stirring ntil sauce thickens, and season to taste with salt and pepper. Return mussels to the pan and gently reheat. Spoon into shells and sprinkle with chopped parsley.

Opposite page: Smoked Salmon Appetisers, recipe above.

Eric Wilson 1911-1946
Abstract - The Kitchen
Stove, 1943
Oil, paper on plywood 145.5 x 79.7cm
Gift of the New South Wales
Travelling Art Scholarship
Committee 1946
Art Gallery of New South Wales

SALMON MOUSSE
Serves 4-6

INGREDIENTS

6 teaspoons gelatine
¼ cup hot water
½ cup evaporated milk
  or cream
¼ cup vinegar or lemon
  juice
½ teaspoon dry mustard
½ teaspoon salt
¼ teaspoon freshly
  ground black pepper
Pinch of nutmeg
1 x 220 g can salmon
1 medium cucumber,
  peeled, grated, and
  thoroughly drained
1 teaspoon caster sugar
¼ cup hot water
½ cup tomato juice
2 medium celery stalks,
  finely chopped
4 shallots, finely chopped

Sour cream dressing
⅔ cup sour cream
1 teaspoon horseradish
  relish
1 teaspoon snipped
  chives 1 teaspoon
  chopped parsley
Pinch of salt
Pinch of cayenne pepper
1 teaspoon vinegar

METHOD

Sprinkle 3 teaspoons of the gelatine into ¼ cup of the hot water, stirring until thoroughly dissolved. Leave to cool slightly. Whisk the evaporated milk with the vinegar or lemon juice, the mustard, salt, black pepper, and nutmeg. Stir in the cooled gelatine. Add the flaked undrained salmon and the cucumber, mixing well. Pour into a mould that has been rinsed with cold water. Put in the refrigerator and leave until set. Meanwhile, dissolve the remaining 3 teaspoons of gelatine and the caster sugar in the remaining ¼ cup of hot water.

Stir in the tomato juice, celery, and shallots. Carefully spoon over the set layer of salmon.

Chill for at least 4 hours. Carefully turn out on to a platter and serve with the dressing.

Sour cream dressing: Mix all ingredients together.

COROMANDEL PRAWNS
Serves 4-5

INGREDIENTS
60g (2oz) butter
2 teaspoons curry
  powder
4 shallots, sliced
1 clove garlic, crushed
1 capsicum, sliced
¾ cup evaporated milk
1 tablespoon tomato
  paste
2 teaspoons soy sauce
½ cup sour cream
1 tablespoon dry sherry
750g (1½lb) prawns,
  shelled
1 x 250g packet frozen
  spinach, thawed

METHOD
Melt butter, add curry powder, shallots, garlic and capsicum
and cook for a few minutes until softened. Stir in
evaporated milk, tomato paste and soy sauce and cook
gently 3-4 minutes.

Add sour cream, sherry and prawns and stir until evenly
mixed and hot. Do not cook any longer at this stage.

Press water out of spinach and cook until tender.
Drain, place on serving dish and top with the curried
prawns. Serve with rice or lots of crusty bread.

SALMON BAKE
Serves 4

INGREDIENTS
8 boiled new potatoes
1 leek, sliced
1 x 185g can salmon,
  drained
3 eggs
1½ cups milk
1 tablespoon chopped
fresh dill
Salt and pepper

METHOD
Slice potatoes and place alternate layers in a greased
ovenproof dish together with leek and salmon.

Beat eggs and milk together. Stir in dill, salt and pepper
to taste. Pour into ovenproof dish.

Bake in a moderately hot oven until set, about 30
minutes. Delicious with carrot salad.

*Right: Coromandel
Prawns, recipe above*

CRAB TARTLETS
Makes aout 24

INGREDIENTS
2 cups plain flour
½ teaspoon baking
    powder
Pinch of salt
155g (5oz) butter,
    chopped
1 egg yolk, mixed with
    3 tablespoons cold
    water
1 x 155 g can crab,
    drained and flaked
60g (2oz) Swiss cheese,
    shredded
½ cup sour cream
1 tablespoon mayonnaise
1 egg, beaten
⅓ cup cream
Salt
Pinch of cayenne pepper
Pinch of nutmeg
1 tablespoon finely
    chopped parsley

METHOD
Sift the flour, baking powder, and salt into a mixing bowl. Add the butter and rub until the mixture resembles breadcrumbs. Add the egg yolk and water and mix to a firm dough (add a little more water if too dry). Wrap in plastic and chill in the refrigerator for about 30 minutes. Roll out the dough to a thickness of 5 mm (¼ in) and cut into rounds to fit into patty tins. Line the tins with the pastry and prick the bases very lightly.

Mix the crab with the cheese and spoon into the pastry cases. Mix the sour cream with mayonnaise, egg, cream, salt to taste, cayenne pepper, nutmeg, and parsley. Spoon over the crab mixture. Bake in a moderately hot oven until the pastry has browned and the filling has set. Carefully remove from the patty tins and serve warm or cold.

OYSTERS KILPATRICK
Serves 4

INGREDIENTS
½ cup tomato sauce
1 tablespoon
Worcestershire sauce
Juice of 1 medium
    lemon
24 oysters on the shell
Salt and pepper
48 small bacon strips

METHOD
Combine sauces and lemon juice. Pour over each oyster. Cover with two bacon strips. Grill quickly until the bacon is crisp.

TROUT ALMONDINE
Serves 4

INGREDIENTS
4 medium trout
Salt
Plain flour
Salt and pepper
125g (4oz) butter
2 teaspoons lemon juice
Freshly ground pepper
⅓ cup blanched
   almonds, toasted and
   split into halves
Lemon wedges

METHOD
Trim the fins of each trout close to the body, leaving the head and tails intact.

Sprinkle the inside of the trout with salt and toss in the flour seasoned with salt and pepper.

Melt half the butter in a frying pan. Add the fish and cook until browned underneath.

Turn and brown the other side.

Carefully lift the fish on to a heated serving platter and keep warm. Add the rest of the butter to the pan with the lemon juice, pepper, and almonds. Cook, stirring, for 2-3 minutes. Pour over the fish and serve at once with the lemon wedges. Serve with salads.

BAKED FISH WITH HERB STUFFING
Serves 4-6

INGREDIENTS
1 large snapper or other
   whole fish
125g (4oz) butter
2 cups bread cubes
4 rashers of bacon,
   chopped
1 small clove garlic,
   crushed
1 stick of celery, sliced
3 shallots, finely
   chopped
1 tablespoon chopped
   fresh thyme, or 1
   teaspoon dried
Salt and freshly ground
   pepper
A little melted butter
Sliced limes or lemons
   to garnish

METHOD
Wipe cavity of fish and place fish on an oiled baking dish. Heat butter in a large pan, add bread cubes and fry until crisp and golden. Remove from pan and set aside to cool.

Place bacon in the same pan, and fry until the fat runs. Add garlic, celery and shallots and cook until soft, about 5 minutes. Combine with bread cubes, herbs, salt and pepper.

Spoon filling into the fish and brush fish with melted butter. Bake in a preheated moderate oven for about ¾ hour, or until flesh is white and opaque and flakes easily when tested with a fork. To serve, cut fish into slices and serve each with a spoonful of herbed bread stuffing. Garnish with lime or lemon slices.

Following pages: Pan Fried Trout, freshly caught in the Snowy Mountains, or some bubbling high-country stream, makes a heavenly outdoor meal. In our photograph, it is served with new potato salad and baby beetroot tossed in mayonnaise and herbs. Trout Almondine, recipe above, is a more sophisticated presentation of this delectable fish.

SKEWERED PRAWNS WITH CHILLI MAYONNAISE AND AVOCADO CREAM

Serves 2

INGREDIENTS

18 medium-sized green
   king prawns
4 tablespoons vegetable
   oil
1 tablespoon lemon juice
½ teaspoon dried
   tarragon
2 zucchini, sliced

Chilli Mayonnaise
¼ cup whole egg
   mayonnaise
1 tablespoon tomato
   sauce
¼ teaspoon ground
   chillies

Avocado cream
1 ripe avocado
1 clove garlic, crushed
2 tablespoons whole egg
   mayonnaise

METHOD

Shell prawns and place in a bowl. Mix together oil, lemon
juice and tarragon.

   Pour over prawns and mix well. Thread onto 2 skewers
with alternate slices of zucchini.

   Brush with the marinade.

   Grill, turning often and brushing with remaining
marinade until prawns turn pink.

   Serve with saffron rice, Chilli Mayonnaise and Avocado
Cream.

Chilli mayonnaise: Mix all ingredients together.

Avocado cream: Mash avocado and stir in garlic and
mayonnaise.

*Opposite page: Skewered
Prawns with Chilli
Mayonnaise and Avocado
Cream, recipe above.*

BARBECUED FISH IN FOIL
Serves 4

INGREDIENTS
1kg (2lb) snapper,
  bream, or jewfish
Garlic salt
Lemon pepper
1 tablespoon butter
Salt
2 tablespoons chopped
  shallots
¾ cup chopped
  mushrooms
2 tablespoons chopped
  parsley
1 medium lemon

METHOD
Make three diagonal incisions about 2.5cm (1in) apart on each side of the fish, in the thickest part. Sprinkle inside of fish with garlic salt and lemon pepper. Brush both sides of the fish with melted butter and sprinkle with salt and lemon pepper.

Melt butter and gently fry the shallots and chopped mushrooms until softened. Stir in parsley. Spoon mixture into cavity of fish and add two or three slices of lemon.

Secure opening with small skewers.

Lightly butter a piece of heavy foil large enough to enclose the fish. Put fish in centre and squeeze over juice from rest of lemon. Bring edges of foil up and fold loosely over fish enclosing it completely. Barbecue until tender when tested with a fork.

Still Life with Fish
Arthur Murch
Oil on board 33.5 x 44cm
Bathurst Regional Art Gallery

x 3kg (6lb) goose 21/2 tablespoons plain flour 3 tablespoons brandy 1
ablespoons butter 1large onion, chopped 2 Granny Smith apples, peele
day-old bread, toasted in the oven 2 teaspoons finely grated lemo
easpoon dried thyme Salt and pepper to taste method Make the stuf
ith damp paper towels. Remove the oil sac from the parsonís nose, usi
secure with poultry pins. Truss the bird, then wipe over with paper
a lightly oiled baking dish. Put the dish over high heat and sear the
15 minutes. Baste, cover with foil, and reduce the temperature to m
the cooking time. Transfer to a heated serving platter, remove th
ablespoons of juice from the pan, add the remaining tablespoon of flo

stock made from neck and giblets of goose, or chicken stock Stuffing
, and diced 1 1/2 cups chopped stoned soft prunes 31/2 cups small cub
/4 cup chopped parsley 1 teaspoon snipped fresh thyme leaves or 1
nove excess fat from the inside of the goose. Wipe inside and outsi
en scissors. Fill the cavity loosely with the stuffing. Sew up the openir
o dry thoroughly. Sprinkle 1 1/2å tablespoons of the flour over and pr
rm the brandy, set alight, and pour over the goose. Roast in a hot ove
Roast for 21/2 hours, removing the foil about 30 minutes before the er
ing string, and keep warm while you make the gravy. Pour all but
tir over medium heat until browned, scraping up the pan juices. Slow

CHICKEN MARYLAND
Serves 4-8

INGREDIENTS
½ cup flour
1 teaspoon salt
½ teaspoon ground
    pepper
1 egg
2 tablespoons water
1 x 1.25-1.5kg (2½-3lb)
    chicken, cut in 8
    pieces
2 cups fine dry
    breadcrumbs
Oil for frying
Tomatoes
Pineapple slices
Bananas
Potatoes
Sweetcorn
Green peas
Watercress or parsley

METHOD
Mix the flour with the salt and pepper. Lightly beat the egg in a shallow bowl with the water. Coat the chicken pieces with the seasoned flour, dip in egg mixture and roll in breadcrumbs.

Heat oil in a heavy frying pan and fry the chicken gently about 20 minutes, turning often with tongs, until crisp and brown and cooked. Drain on paper towels and keep warm. Serve chicken portions on individual plates with traditional American Chicken Maryland accompaniments such as grilled tomato halves, pineapple slices and bananas, little sweetcorn patties or balls, potato balls or chips, green peas and watercress or parsley garnish.

ITALIAN LEMON CHICKEN
Serves 4-5

INGREDIENTS
1.5kg (3lb) small
    chicken pieces
Salt and pepper
½ teaspoon dried
    rosemary
¼ cup vegetable oil
1 clove garlic, crushed
½ cup dry white wine
3 eggs
2 tablespoons lemon
    juice

METHOD
Sprinkle chicken pieces with salt, pepper and rosemary. Heat oil and brown chicken on both sides. Cook until tender.

Stir in garlic and wine. Beat eggs with lemon juice and pour over the chicken stirring all the time. The egg must not be allowed to cook, just to thicken. Serve at once.

A Second World War newcomer from the United States and a surprise to palates not familiar with the sweet taste of fruit with chicken, Chicken Maryland was often served in restaurants with coleslaw, and followed by a Banana Split for dessert. Chicken Maryland, recipe page 152, with corn fritters, fried banana, pineapple, stuffed tomato, potato puffs and peas.

CHICKEN PROVENÇALE

Serves 4

INGREDIENTS

2 tablespoons of
   vegetable oil
1 tablespoon butter
1.25kg (2½lb) small
   chicken pieces
2 tablespoons brandy
¾ cup dry white wine
4 tomatoes, peeled
8 small onions, peeled
1 apple, peeled and
   diced
½ cup green olives
1 teaspoon curry
powder
½ teaspoon dried thyme
Salt to taste
250g (8oz) button
   mushrooms
Chopped parsley
Snipped chives

METHOD

Heat oil and butter together. Add chicken pieces and
brown all over. Pour off remaining oil and butter and
reserve for cooking the mushrooms. Pour brandy over
chicken and flambé.

Add wine, tomatoes, onions, apple, olives, curry powder,
thyme and salt. Cover with a tight-fitting lid and cook
gently until tender, about 30–35 minutes, adding a little
extra wine if necessary.

Cook mushrooms in the reserved oil and butter, add to
chicken and sprinkle top with parsley and chives. Serve
with ribbon noodles.

WARM CHICKEN SALAD

Serves 4

INGREDIENTS

4 boned chicken breasts
2 tablespoons lemon
   juice
2 tablespoons butter
1 cup sliced celery
¼ cup walnut pieces
2 tablespoons soft blue
   vein cheese
¼ cup French dressing
Lettuce leaves and
   chives

METHOD

Place chicken breasts and lemon juice in a bowl and
refrigerate for 1 hour.

Melt butter and cook chicken until golden brown
Drain and slice. Combine celery, walnuts, cheese and
dressing. Arrange lettuce leaves on 4 individual plates, top
with the warm chicken and then celery mixture. Sprinkle
with snipped chives and serve.

*Opposite page:
Chicken Provençale,
recipe above.*

CHICKEN INDIENNE

INGREDIENTS

1 x 1.5-2kg (3-4lb)
  chicken
2½ cups water
2 strips lemon rind
1 onion, chopped
6 whole allspice
6 peppercorns
1 sprig thyme, 2 sprigs
  parsley, 1 bay leaf,
  tied together
1½ teaspoons salt
Sauce Inienne:
(recipe follows)

METHOD

Place chicken in heavy saucepan with water, lemon rind, onion, allspice, peppercorns, bunch of herbs and salt. Bring to boil and simmer, covered, for 45 minutes or until tender.

When cool, remove chicken from stock and take meat from bones. Discard skin and cut flesh into thick slices.

Reserve 2 cups of stock, and skim any fat from surface.

Sauce indienne: Melt 60g (2oz) butter, add 1 tablespoon curry powder and 2 tablespoons flour and stir until smooth over low heat. Cook together for a few minutes. Slowly stir in 2 cups of stock from cooked chicken and stir constantly over moderate heat until sauce thickens. Add 1 tablespoon redcurrant jelly, beating into the sauce. Allow mixture to cool, whisking once or twice. Mix in ½ cup cream, then fold in the chicken pieces and add salt and white pepper to taste. Serve cold. This dish makes an ideal part of a cold buffet, with rice and salads.

TURKEY AND MUSHROOM PIE

Serves 7-8

INGREDIENTS

90g (3oz) butter
1 onion, chopped
250g (8oz) mushrooms,
  sliced
¼ cup flour
Salt and pepper
1 cup chicken stock
¾ cup cream
4 cups cooked, diced
  turkey
250g (8oz) puff pastry

METHOD

Cook butter, onion and mushrooms until soft. Stir in flour, salt and pepper and cook 2 minutes. Add stock, cream and turkey and stir until boiling. Place in a pie dish and cover with rolled out pastry. Seal edges and make slits in top for steam to escape.

Brush with milk and bake in a hot oven 20 minutes until browned.

Following pages:
Picnic Egg and Chicken
Pie, recipe above.

The Lesson 1912
Oil on canvas 182.2 x 111.8cm
Felton Bequest 1925
National Gallery of Victoria

The tray of tea things on the table and the gentle warmth of the woman and her child in this charming painting depicts a way of life that has completely disappeared. The custom of drinking tea in the afternoon was brought to the colonies by the English and became known to Australians as afternoon tea.

Because of the faster pace of modern life after the Second World War and the fact that so many women work, it declined in popularity. However, it is becoming fashionable again among those with leisure time to spare. In the past, it was a stylish ritual and to define the status of the household where an afternoon tea was held, there were fine displays of napery, silver and china. Thin bread and butter, little sandwiches, small snacks such as scones and crumpets, and cakes of all shapes and sizes provided agreeable accompaniments to tea, conversation and gossip. For Australian workers, morning and afternoon tea breaks are still essential; a cup of tea and a biscuit offer a welcome escape from routine.

CHERRIED QUAIL

Serves 4

INGREDIENTS

4 quails
4 small pieces of orange
  rind, with pith
  removed
6 tablespoons butter,
  approximately
4 parsley sprigs
2 small onions, halved
Fresh or dried thyme
Pork fat or bacon
Salt and pepper
⅔ cup water
½ cup dry white wine
½ cup stoned canned
  cherries

Bread sauce: (optional)
1 small onion, finely
chopped
1 cup milk
1 bay leaf
4 peppercorns
1 cup soft white
breadcrumbs
Salt
1 teaspoon butter

METHOD

Wipe the birds inside and out with paper towels. Put in the cavity of each a small piece of orange rind, about 2 teaspoons of the butter, a parsley sprig, an onion half, and a good pinch of thyme. Tie the legs and wings of each bird close to its body with string. Cover the breast of each with pork fat or bacon and tie with string. Melt 3 tablespoons of the remaining butter in a large baking dish, add the quails, and brown them all over.

Cover the dish, put in a very hot oven, and roast for 20 minutes, basting several times with the fat and juices in the dish. Remove the pork fat or bacon and the trussing string, baste the birds well, and sprinkle with salt and pepper. Lower the oven temperature to moderate and return the birds for 5 minutes. Remove the birds to a heated serving platter and keep hot while you make the gravy.

Add the water and wine to the dish and stir over brisk heat, scraping up the pan juices, for 2–3 minutes. Stir in the remaining tablespoon of butter and season with salt and pepper to taste. Add the cherries and heat through. Serve the birds with the gravy and bread sauce.

Bread sauce: Put the onion in a saucepan with the milk, bay leaf, and peppercorns.

Cook over gentle heat for 20 minutes. Strain and then mix in the breadcrumbs and salt to taste. Simmer 3–4 minutes. Stir in the butter.

PICNIC EGG AND CHICKEN PIE
Serves 8

INGREDIENTS

1 cup plain flour
1 cup self-raising flour
1 teaspoon salt
155g (5oz) butter, chopped
1 egg yolk, lightly beaten
Cold water
8 chicken breasts
1 ham steak
6 spring onions, finely chopped
1 tablespoon chopped parsley
1 teaspoon mixed dried herbs
Pepper and salt
5 hard-boiled eggs
Beaten egg yolk for glazing

METHOD

Sift the flours and salt into a mixing bowl. Rub the butter in with fingertips until mixture resembles breadcrumbs. Add the egg yolk with enough cold water to form a firm dough. Chill for about 30 minutes.

Take two-thirds and roll out to fit into a 23cm (9in) greased springform tin. Shred chicken breasts and cube the ham steak. In a bowl, mix with the spring onions, parsley, mixed herbs and pepper and salt. Spread half of the mixture into the pastry case. Arrange the whole shelled hard boiled eggs over the top and cover with the remaining mixture. Roll out the rest of the pastry to form a cover. Moisten the edges of the pastry case and place cover on top, pressing edges together to seal. Decorate with scraps, brush with beaten egg yolk. Cut two small slits in top to allow steam to escape. Bake in a moderately hot oven for 30 minutes. Reduce heat to moderate and bake a further 1 hour, covering the top with foil if it browns too quickly. Cool and chill in the refrigerator. Serve with salads.

Following pages:
Turkey Tetrazzini, recipe
page 168.

Helen Eager

9am 1977
Lithograph 46 x 37cm
Bathurst Regional Art Gallery

DUCK WITH GREEN PEPPERCORNS
Serves 4

INGREDIENTS
1 x 2.5kg (4½lb) duck
Salt and pepper
2 tablespoons chopped
  parsley

Peppercorn sauce
1 small onion, finely
chopped
4 tablespoons red wine
  vinegar
1 teaspoon chopped
  fresh tarragon or ½
  teaspoon dried
  tarragon
1 teaspoon snipped
  fresh thyme or ½
  teaspoon dried thyme
3 tablespoons canned
  green peppercorns
2 teaspoons French
  mustard
1½ cups stock made
  with duck neck and
  giblets, or chicken
  stock

METHOD
Remove excess fat from the inside of the duck. Wipe inside
and outside with damp paper towels. Sprinkle salt and
pepper inside. Truss the duck and put it, breast side up, on a
rack in a baking dish. Roast in a moderately hot oven for
15 minutes and then prick all around the tail end to release
the fat. Continue roasting for 1¾ hours, or until tender
when tested, basting occasionally.

While the duck is cooking, make the sauce. Remove the
duck to a heated platter and keep warm. Spoon as much fat
as possible from the baking dish and discard this fat. Stir the
drippings from the baking dish into the peppercorn sauce.
Stir until reheated, add the parsley, and simmer for 1 minute.
Carve the duck into serving portions, spoon a little of the
sauce over, and serve the rest separately.

Peppercorn sauc: Put the onion in a small saucepan with
the vinegar, tarragon, and thyme. Bring to the boil, stirring,
then continue boiling gently until the liquid has evaporated.

Rinse the peppercorns in cold water and add to the
onion with the mustard and stock. Stir until boiling, then
cook gently until reduced a little.

Following pages:
Duckling Nouvelle with
Strawberry Coulis, recipe
page 171.

TURKEY TETRAZZINI
Serves 4-5

INGREDIENTS
250 g (8 oz) pink, green
  or white tagliatelle or
  a mixture of all three
4 tablespoons butter
125 g (4 oz)
  mushrooms, thinly
  sliced
1 small onion, grated
¼ cup plain flour
1 cup evaporated milk
1½ cups chicken stock
2 tablespoons dry sherry
Salt and pepper
1 small green and 1
  small red capsicum,
  cut into short thin
  strips
2 cups diced cooked
  turkey
½ cup grated Parmesan
  cheese

METHOD
Cook the spaghetti in plenty of boiling salted water until tender. Drain and arrange in a greased ovenproof dish. Melt half the butter, add the mushrooms, and gently fry until softened. Add the rest of the butter and the onion and cook for 20 seconds. Stir in the flour, and cook for 1 minute. Slowly stir in the evaporated milk and the stock and cook, stirring, until boiling. Add the sherry, season with salt and pepper, and simmer for 1–2 minutes.

Drop the strips of capsicum into a small pan of cold water and slowly bring to the boil. Drain and add to the sauce. Pour half the sauce over the spaghetti, mixing in.

Add the turkey to the rest of the sauce and pour into the dish. Sprinkle with the grated cheese and bake in a moderately hot oven for about 15 minutes. Serve with a green salad.

HONEY DUCKLING
Serves 4-5

INGREDIENTS
1 x 2.25 kg (4½ lb)
  duckling
Salt and pepper
Grated rind 1 orange
2 cloves garlic, crushed
1 small onion, chopped
  finely
3 tablespoons soy sauce
3 tablespoons sherry
2 tablespoons honey

METHOD
Rub inside duck with salt, pepper and orange rind. Pierce all over with a skewer and bake on a rack in a baking dish in a moderate oven.

Combine all remaining ingredients and brush over duck while cooking.

Cook until tender, about 2 hours.

Opposite page:
Chicken with Cheese
Sauce, recipe page 170.

CHICKEN KEBABS WITH PEANUT SAUCE
Serves 4

INGREDIENTS
8 chicken liver halves
2 bacon rashers, rind removed
8 small pieces of chicken breast
8 small onions, peeled
8 tomato wedges
8 pineapple pieces
4 green capsicum strips
½ cup vegetable oil
2 tablespoons orange juice
1 tablespoon lemon juice
1 teaspoon soy sauce
1 teaspoon brown sugar
½ teaspoon ground ginger
Few drops hot pepper sauce

METHOD
Wrap the chicken livers in small pieces of the bacon and alternate on 4 skewers with all the other foods. Mix together the remaining ingredients for the marinade and brush over skewers. Grill over hot coals, or under a griller, brushing now and again with the marinade. Cook on both sides until tender. Serve with saffron rice and peanut sauce.

Peanut sauce: Mix together ½ cup sour cream, 4 tablespoons chopped salted peanuts and ½ teaspoon onion powder.

CHICKEN WITH CHEESE SAUCE
Serves 8

INGREDIENTS
2 kg (4 lb) chicken pieces
Salt and pepper
½ cup chicken stock
1 leek, sliced thinly
1 cup thickened cream
250 g (8 oz) blue vein cheese, crumbled
½ cup sour cream
¼ cup dry vermouth
½ cup walnut pieces

METHOD
Sprinkle chicken with salt and pepper and place in a baking dish.

Bake in a hot oven 25 minutes, turning once. Pour in the chicken stock, spoon over chicken and bake another 10 minutes. Place chicken in an ovenproof dish.

Place baking dish over medium heat on the stove and remove excess fat. Add leek, cream and cheese and stir until cheese melts. Simmer for a few minutes then stir in sour cream and vermouth.

Pour over the chicken and sprinkle with walnuts. Cover and bake 10 minutes.

DUCKLING NOUVELLE

Serves 2

INGREDIENTS

2 duckling breasts
2 tablespoons butter
2 tablespoons strawberry
  vinegar or white wine
½ cup strawberries
Black pepper
1 avocado, sliced
1 mango, sliced
1 punnet salad cress
2 tablespoons pecan nuts
Extra strawberries
Witlof leaves
1 red capsicum, peeled
  and cut into julienne
  strips
Cherry tomatoes

METHOD

Sauté duckling breasts in the butter until cooked. Put aside to cool. Skim off fat and deglaze pan with the vinegar or white wine. Strain and put in blender or food processor with ½ cup strawberries and black pepper, to form a sauce or coulis. Taste and add a little sugar if necessary. Pour a pool of coulis onto 2 plates. Slice duckling breasts into fan shapes and place beside coulis on each plate. Arrange other ingredients decoratively to form a pretty picture, using your imagination.

gredients 1 x 2.5kg (5lb) leg of lamb 90g (3oz) butter 1 medium onion
hopped fresh rosemary (or 1/2 teaspoon dried) 2 teaspoons chopped
round pepper Gravy 11/2 tablespoons plain flour 11/2 cups stock made
one. Heat the butter and fry onion until soft and golden. Skin and c
rowned. Remove from heat and add breadcrumbs, herbs and salt and
ith string. Season with salt and pepper, arrange on a greased rack i
bout 2 hours for well done lamb, basting now and then with juices th
rving.Gravy: Pour off all but 2 tablespoons of drippings in pan, an
ontinue stirring until gravy is smooth and thickened. Taste for seasor
utter 1 medium onion, finely chopped 2 lamb kidneys 2 cups soft, wh

Meat and game

chopped 2 lamb kidneys 2 cups soft, white breadcrumbs 2 teaspoon

e (or 1/2 teaspoon dried) 2 teaspoons chopped parsley Salt and finel

nb bone method Ask the butcher to bone the lamb for you and save th

kidneys and cut into small dice. Add to the pan and stir until lightl

taste. Allow to cool a little, then stuff lamb and tie into a neat shap

g dish, and place in a preheated moderate oven.Roast uncovered fo

t in the pan. Allow to rest for 20 minutes before removing string an

flour over low heat. When well blended, gradually stir in stock an

strain into a gravy boat. ingredients 1 x 2.5kg (5lb) leg of lamb 90g (30z

crumbs 2 teaspoons chopped fresh rosemary (or 1/2 teaspoon dried)

TEXAS HOTPOT
Serves 2-3

INGREDIENTS
250g (8oz) thickly
  sliced bacon
2 onions, sliced
1 clove garlic, crushed
1 x 400g can tomatoes
4-6 small potatoes,
  sliced
Salt and pepper
3-4 fresh or frozen
  corn cobs

METHOD
Cook bacon in its own fat until browned. Remove. Add
onion and garlic to bacon fat and cook a few minutes. Add
a little butter if necessary.

Stir in undrained tomatoes, sliced potatoes, salt and
pepper to taste and the bacon.

Cook gently with the lid on 10-15 minutes.

Slice the corn cobs and press into the hotpot, adding a
small amount of vegetable stock if necessary. Cover pot and
cook until corn is tender, about 10 minutes.

SPICY GLAZED PORK
Serves 4-5

INGREDIENTS
1.5kg (3lb) pork
  shoulder
2 teaspoons curry
  powder
1 teaspoon ground
  ginger
1 clove garlic, crushed
1 teaspoon dried thyme
Salt to taste
2 carrots, sliced
1 parsnip, sliced
1 turnip, cut into pieces
1 leek, washed and
  sliced
2 cups beef stock
3 teaspoons arrowroot

METHOD
Cut pork in half if desired. Combine curry, ginger, garlic,
thyme and salt. Rub into pork and place in an ovenproof dish.

Place the vegetables around the meat and pour over the
stock. Cover with lid and bake in a moderate oven until
meat is tender.

Carefully pour the stock into a saucepan, stir in blended
arrowroot and cook until boiling and thickened. Pour over
meat in dish and serve.

*Opposite page: Texas
Hotpot, recipe above.*

VENISON WITH WALNUTS
Serves 6-8

INGREDIENTS
1kg (2lb) stewing venison (cut from shoulder)

2 tablespoons plain flour

1 teaspoon dried mixed herbs

2 medium onions, finely chopped

2 large tomatoes, peeled and chopped

Salt and freshly ground pepper

Small piece cinnamon stick

5 pickled walnuts, sliced

2 teaspoons Angostura bitters

¾ cup red wine

Extra walnut slices and chopped parsley to garnish

METHOD
Remove any sinews from venison, cut meat into cubes and roll lightly in flour.

Arrange the cubes in a greased ovenproof dish in layers, sprinkling each layer with herbs, onions and tomatoes and seasoning with salt and pepper as you go.

Add the cinnamon stick and pickled walnut slices. Combine bitters and red wine and pour into the dish. Cover tightly and cook in a moderate oven for 1½- 2 hours or until venison is fork tender. Serve topped with a few pickled walnut slices and chopped parsley.

VEAL CORDON BLEU
Serves 4

INGREDIENTS
4 thin veal steaks

2 tablespoons vegetable oil

Salt

French mustard

4 ham slices

4 slices Swiss or Emmenthal cheese

METHOD
Cook veal steaks in hot oil for 1 minute on each side. Remove and place on grilling tray. Sprinkle with salt to taste and spread with mustard. Cover with a slice of ham, then with a slice of cheese.

Grill under high heat until cheese is bubbly and golden.

MEATBALLS WITH GREEN PEPPERCORN SAUCE
Serves 4

INGREDIENTS
500g (1lb) minced beef
1 egg
½ cup soft breadcrumbs
1 tablespoon French
    mustard
Salt and pepper to taste
3 tablespoons vegetable
    oil
185g (6oz) fresh
    mushrooms, sliced
1 x 25g packet brown
    sauce mix
1¼ cups evaporated milk
1 tablespoon dry sherry
2 tablespoons green
    peppercorns
Chopped parsley

METHOD
Mix together minced beef, egg, breadcrumbs, mustard, salt and pepper and form into balls.

Heat oil, add meatballs and brown all over, shaking pan frequently. Add mushrooms and continue cooking until meatballs are cooked.

Make up the sauce mix with evaporated milk, stir in sherry and peppercorns.

Pour over meatballs and sprinkle with chopped parsley.

VEAL ESCALOPES WITH SMOKED HAM
Serves 4-6

INGREDIENTS
6 thin veal steaks
Salt and pepper
1-2 tablespoons
    chopped fresh sage
6 slices smoked ham
Flour
60g (2oz) butter
½ cup rosé or light
    white wine

METHOD
Season meat with salt and pepper and sprinkle evenly with sage. Place a slice of ham on each veal steak and fasten with a wooden toothpick. Coat lightly in flour.

Cook slowly in the butter. Pour over the wine and stir vigorously to combine with the butter. Remove picks and serve with sautéed potatoes.

AUSSIE MEAT PIES
Serves 4

INGREDIENTS

250g (8oz) shortcrust
  pastry
1 tablespoon butter
1 onion, finely chopped
250g (8oz) minced beef
1 tablespoon plain flour
2 tablespoons tomato
  sauce
1 tablespoon
  Worcestershire sauce
2 tablespoons water
Salt and pepper
Beaten egg for glazing

METHOD

Roll pastry out thinly, cut into rounds and line four 10 cm
(4 in) pie tins.

Meanwhile make filling. Heat the butter and gently fry
the onion until transparent. Add beef and stir until
browned. Stir in flour, sauces, water, salt and pepper, and
bring to boil. Remove from heat and cool. Divide filling
between the 4 tins, cut 4 rounds from remaining pastry and
cover each pie, crimping edges. Make a vent with a skewer
in the centre of each and decorate with pastry trimmings.
Brush with beaten egg. Stand tins on a baking tray and bake
in a hot oven 20 minutes until cooked.

Serve with tomato sauce or, for a more substantial meal,
with creamy mashed potatoes and peas.

STEAK AND OYSTER PIE
Serves 6

INGREDIENTS

1kg (2lb) chuck steak,
  fat removed, cubed
375g (12oz) ox kidney,
  skin and fat removed,
  chopped
Flour seasoned with salt
  and pepper
60g (2oz) butter
2 onions, chopped
1¼ cups beef stock
½ teaspoon dried thyme
Salt and pepper
Dash of Worcestershire
  sauce
1 tablespoon chopped
  parsley
2 dozen fresh oysters
375g (12oz) puff pastry
Egg yolk or milk for
  glazing

METHOD

Lightly coat the steak and kidney pieces with seasoned
flour. In a large wide heavy saucepan, brown all over in the
heated butter. Add the onions and cook 2-3 minutes,
stirring. Pour off fat, add beef stock and stir until nearly
boiling. Add the thyme, salt, pepper and Worcestershire
sauce. Cook gently about 1½ hours or until meat is almost
tender.

Mix in parsley. Transfer to a pie dish and put aside. When
cold, add the oysters.

Roll out the pastry to an oblong a little larger than the
dish, cut narrow strips from ends. Moisten edges of pie dish,
top with pastry strips. Brush with water and top with rest
of the pastry. Press edges together, trim off excess. Make 2
or 3 slits in top and decorate with pastry trimmings. Brush
over with beaten egg yolk or milk. Bake in a very hot oven
for 15 minutes, reduce to moderate and bake another
20-25 minutes.

*The meat pie came to
us from England and
ultimately became a
popular commercial
food favourite here.
The pie with
tomato sauce is
sometimes called our
national dish.*

*Its portability
lends extra charm to
its often dubious
contents. Homemade
meat pies were sold
in the streets of
Sydney and
Melbourne in the
very early days.
During the
Depression a few
shillings would pay
for a pie and a
picture show. Our
Aussie Meat Pie,
recipe above, is a
version of the classic
original and offers the
flavours and succulent
textures which have
made it so popular
for so long.*

CRUSTY LEG OF LAMB
Serves 6

INGREDIENTS
1 x 1.5-2kg (3-4lb) leg lamb

1 egg yolk

3 tablespoons butter, melted

1 cup cornflake crumbs

1 tablespoon sesame seeds

Salt to taste

½ teaspoon seasoned mixed herbs

1 small onion, sliced

METHOD
Remove excess fat from lamb, brush top of surface with a little of the egg yolk.

Mix together butter, cornflake crumbs, sesame seeds, salt, seasoned mixed herbs and half the remaining egg yolk.

Press mixture firmly over top of lamb, break onion slices into rings and arrange in a pattern over the crumb surface, pressing with the palm of your hand. Brush the onion rings with rest of egg yolk.

Put into a baking dish and bake in a moderate oven about 1½ hours, or until done to your liking. When the crust becomes golden and crisp, cover with foil for the rest of the cooking time.

RICE AND SAUSAGE CASSEROLE
Serves 6

INGREDIENTS
500g (1lb) sausages oil

1 large onion finely chopped

1 small green capsicum, diced

3 large tomatoes, peeled and chopped

1½ cups long-grain rice

3 mushroom stock-cubes, crumbled

3 cups hot water

salt and pepper

1 cup cooked green peas

METHOD
Put the sausages in a saucepan with enough cold water to cover and slowly bring to the boil. Rinse in cold water and drain thoroughly.

Heat oil and brown sausages quickly all over. Drain on paper towels and cut crossways into quarters.

Heat a little more oil and fry the onion gently in the pan until softened. Add the capsicum and tomatoes and cook, stirring, for 2or 3 minutes. Add the sausage sections and the rice, stirring well.

Transfer to an oven proof dish. Dissolve the stock-cubes in hot water and pour into the dish. Add salt and pepper, cover with a tight-fitting lid, and cook in a moderately hot oven for 25 minutes, or until the liquid has been absorbed and the rice is tender. Add the green peas, mixing it with a fork, and return to the oven for 5 minutes.

RABBIT TERRINE

Serves 8

INGREDIENTS

Meat from back legs
  and saddles of 2
  rabbits, minced and
  marinated a few hours
  in ¼ cup brandy
2 rabbit or chicken
  livers, finely chopped
500g (1lb) streaky
  pork belly, minced
1 white onion, finely
  chopped and sauteed
  in 1 tablespoon butter
125g (4oz) chopped
  mushrooms
1 teaspoon chopped
  fresh rosemary
1 teaspoon chopped
  parsley
½ cup white wine
Salt and pepper
½ teaspoon ground
  nutmeg
2 tablespoons cream
2 bay leaves
6 rashers bacon, rinds
  removed

METHOD

In a bowl combine all ingredients except bay leaves and
bacon. Line an ovenproof terrine with the bacon, leaving
ends of rashers overlapping sides. Fill terrine with mixture.

Place bay leaves on top and bring overlapping bacon
ends over top. Bake in a baking dish half full of water in a
moderate oven 1 - 1¼ hours or until juices run clear when
tested with skewer. Serve with salad, Herb Toasts and a jug
of Sangria, a refreshing Spanish drink.

Herb toast: French bread slices, rubbed with crushed
garlic, brushed with olive oil sprinkled with fresh or dried
mixed herbs of your choice. Arrange on a baking tray and
in moderate oven until golden and crisp. They will keep
well in an airtight container.

SANGRIA

INGREDIENTS

1½ cups water
1 cup sugar
1 cinnamon stick
2 lemons, sliced
1 bottle red wine
Soda water
Ice
Mint leaves

METHOD

Place water, sugar and cinnamon stick in a saucepan and stir
until boiling and sugar is dissolved. Simmer 5 minutes.

Place lemon slices in a bowl and pour over the syrup.
Allow to stand for a few hours.

Stir in the wine, soda water to taste, ice and mint leaves.
Pour into a jug and serve in wine glasses.

*Following pages:
Rabbit Terrine with
salad, Herb Toasts and
Sangria, recipes above.*

CHINESE BEEF AND VEGETABLES
Serves 8

INGREDIENTS
3 tablespoons vegetable oil

1kg (2lb) lean beef, cut into thin strips

125g (4oz) mushrooms, sliced

1 carrot, cut into thin strips

1 x 230g can water chestnuts, drained

6 shallots, cut into strips

1 large capsicum, cut into strips

1 cup thin strips of celery

250g (8oz) bean sprouts

3 garlic cloves, crushed

2 tablespoons chopped fresh ginger

1 cup chicken stock

1 tablespoon soy sauce

2 tablespoons dry sherry

3 teaspoons arrowroot or cornflour

METHOD
Heat oil. Brown meat and mushrooms quickly. Remove. Add carrot, water chestnuts, shallots, capsicum, celery, bean sprouts, garlic and ginger and stir-fry lightly.

Mix remaining ingredients together, and add to pan, together with meat and mushrooms. Stir until thickened and clear. Serve with rice.

LAMB BURGERS
Serves 4

INGREDIENTS
500g (1lb) minced lamb

1 onion, grated

½ cup soft breadcrumbs

2 tablespoons chopped parsley

1 egg

1 clove garlic, crushed

Salt and pepper to taste

2 tablespoons oil

METHOD
Combine minced lamb with all ingredients and form into fairly large burgers.

Heat oil and cook on both sides until browned. Cook until tender. Burgers should be pink on the inside.

Opposite page:
Chinese Beef and
Vegetables, recipe above.

VEAL ESCALOPES WITH GORGONZOLA SAUCE

Serves 4-6

INGREDIENTS
6 thin veal steaks
Salt and pepper
Flour
2 tablespoons butter
90g (3oz) Gorgonzola
  cheese
1 tablespoon butter
1 tablespoon brandy
½ cup cream

METHOD
Season veal with salt and pepper and dip lightly into flour. Melt the 2 tablespoons butter and cook veal on both sides until lightly browned. Keep warm.

Stir cheese and the 1 tablespoon butter together until cheese melts then add brandy and stir well. Add cream and heat gently. Strain if necessary and pour over the veal steaks.

BEEF IN RED WINE

Serves 4

INGREDIENTS
1kg (2lb) piece of
  roasting beef
Salt and pepper
2 tablespoons oil
2 carrots, sliced
2 onions, cut into
  wedges
1 cup diced celery
2 cloves garlic, crushed
2 tablespoons flour
2 cups red wine
2 peeled tomatoes,
chopped

METHOD
Sprinkle beef with salt and pepper and brown on all sides in the hot oil. Add carrots, onion, celery and garlic and cook a few minutes.

Sprinkle flour over the top, stir in and cook 2-3 minutes. Add wine and tomatoes.

Cover and bake in a moderate oven until tender, about 1 ½ hours.

Continental restaurants, bistros and street cafés proliferated after the Second World War. Scenes, such as the one opposite became commonplace in our cities, and Italian cuisine has always been popular. Top, Veal Escalopes with Smoked Ham, recipe page 177; right, Veal Escalopes with Gorgonzola Sauce, recipe above; below, Italian Lemon Chicken, recipe page 152.

STEAK WITH PEARS
Serves 2

INGREDIENTS
2 T-bone steaks
4 canned pear halves
Melted butter
Ground ginger

Marinade:
¼ cup honey
¼ cup soy sauce
Juice of 1 medium
   lemon
1 cup tomato sauce
Pepper

METHOD
About the steaks are needed, put them in a
shallow dish and spoon the marinade over. Turn the steaks
once while they are marinating. Just before cooking, remove
and drain the steaks. Grill until cooked to your liking.

While the steaks are grilling, brush the pear halves with
melted butter, sprinkle with ginger, and heat through in a
moderately hot oven, or under the griller. Gently heat the
marinade and serve with the meat.
Marinade: Mix together the honey, soy sauce, lemon juice,
tomato sauce and pepper to taste.

DEVILLED PORK CHOPS
Serves 4

INGREDIENTS
4 loin pork chops
Salt and pepper
6 shallots, chopped
1 tablespoon green
   peppercorns
1 cup red wine

METHOD
Season chops with salt and pepper and cook quickly on
both sides until lightly browned.

Add shallots and cook a few minutes. Stir in peppercorns
and wine and cook gently until reduced by half.

Taste for seasoning and serve at once with cooked
vegetables.

Margaret Preston 1875-1963
The Snail 1949
Gouache stencil on black card
29.9 x 21.2cm
purchased 1949
Art Gallery of New South Wales

GOLD COAST RACK OF LAMB
Serves 6

INGREDIENTS

2 racks of lamb, each
  with 6 cutlets
½ cup redcurrant jelly
2 tablespoons pineapple
  juice
1 teaspoon salt
¼ teaspoon pepper

Seasoning:
2 tablespoons butter
1 cup coarse soft
  wholemeal
  breadcrumbs
1 cup fresh or canned
  chopped pineapple
  with juice
1½ tablespoons chopped
  mint
Salt and pepper
½ teaspoon ground or
  1 teaspoon finely
  chopped fresh ginger

Redcurrant Mint Sauce:
1 tablespoon redcurrant
  jelly dissolved with 1
  tablespoon boiling
  water
2 tablespoons red wine
  vinegar
2 tablespoons finely
  chopped mint

METHOD

Remove the fine skin from the fat on the lamb and place
the racks on a baking dish, fat side up. Melt the redcurrant
jelly and pineapple juice over hot water, season with salt
and pepper and brush over cutlets. Bake in a moderately
hot oven for 25 minutes.

Remove from oven and brush again with glaze. Return
to oven and continue baking until done to your liking.

Make gravy in the usual way, using vegetable stock for
liquid. Bake seasoning in oven on a separate greased pie dish.
Seasoning: Heat the butter and toss breadcrumbs in it until
they are golden brown.

Mix lightly with pineapple, mint, salt, pepper and ginger.
Place in dish and cover lightly with foil, removing foil
towards end of cooking. Remove from oven and keep warm
until ready to serve with cutlets. Hand Redcurrant Mint
Sauce separately.
Red currant mint sauce: Mix ingredients together, adding
extra jelly, hot water or vinegar to taste.

Opposite page:
Gold Coast Rack of
Lamb with Pineapple
Seasoning, recipe above.

x 425g can whole peeled tomatoes, chopped, and their liquid Chicken
garlic, crushed 1 medium green capsicum, diced 2 cups long grain
oked ham, diced 250g (8oz) prawns, peeled and deveined 2 breasts of
nd their liquid and add enough stock to make 3 cups. Heat gently
psicum, and fry gently for 1-2 minutes. Add the rice and stir over lo
e ham. Add the boiling tomato mixture, cover tightly, and cook over
dding a little more stock if necessary. Scatter the prawns and chicker
ated through. Sprinkle with Tabasco and chopped parsley, and ser
reshly ground black pepper 1 tablespoon chopped parsley 4 slices of
icken, diced Tabasco Chopped parsley method Measure the tomat

Pasta & rice

water 3 tablespoons butter or oil 1 large onion, finely chopped 1 clou
Freshly ground black pepper 1 tablespoon chopped parsley 4 slices
chicken, diced Tabasco Chopped parsley method Measure the tomatoe
ling. Heat the butter or oil in a large pan, add the onion, garlic, an
or 2-3 minutes. Mix in salt and black pepper to taste, the parsley, an
for 20 minutes, or until the rice is tender and liquid has been absorbe
e top, replace the lid, and return to very low heat until the prawns a
, crushed 1 medium green capsicum, diced 2 cups long grain rice Sa
am, diced 250g (8oz) prawns, peeled and deveined 2 breasts of cooke
their liquid and add enough stock to make 3 cups. Heat gently unt

LAMB PILAF
Serves 4

INGREDIENTS
500g (1lb) boneless
    lamb, diced
90g (3oz) ghee or
    butter
1 onion, chopped
1 carrot, cut into
    julienne strips
Salt and pepper
2 cups uncooked rice
3½ cups boiling
    chicken stock
½ cup raisins
Sliced raw onion
Chopped parsley

METHOD
Brown meat in the ghee or butter. Stir in onion and carrot and cook for a few minutes.

Season to taste with salt and pepper, add rice and stir until coated with ghee.

Pour over the boiling stock, cover with a tight-fitting lid and cook until rice is tender and liquid has been absorbed, about 20 minutes. Add raisins, replace lid and leave until plumped.

Garnish with onion slices and chopped parsley and serve.

TAGLIATELLE WITH MUSSELS
Serves 4 entrées

INGREDIENTS
1kg (2lb) mussels
¼ cup olive oil
1 tablespoon butter
4 tomatoes, peeled
1 clove garlic, crushed
1 onion, chopped finely
Salt and pepper
1 tablespoon chopped
    fresh basil
500g (1lb) tagliatelle,
    cooked
Thin strips shallots or
    zucchini for garnish

METHOD
Wash mussels well and cook in the hot oil until shells have opened. Keep a few for garnish and remove the remaining mussels from their shells. Strain liquid from mussels and reserve. Melt butter, add chopped tomatoes, garlic and onion and cook a few minutes. Stir in mussel liquid and season with salt and pepper to taste. Lastly stir in basil.

Place the hot drained tagliatelle on individual plates. Spoon tomato mixture on top, add the warm mussels in their sheets and garnish with fine strips of shallot or zucchini.

*Opposite page: Lamb
Pilaf, recipe above.*

NOODLES WITH FRESH TOMATO SAUCE
Serves 4

INGREDIENTS
2 onions, chopped

1 cup chopped celery or zucchini

2 tablespoons butter

750g (1½lb) ripe tomatoes, peeled

3 tablespoons tomato paste

1 vegetable stock cube

1 tablespoon chopped fresh basil

½ cup grated Parmesan cheese

1 cup thick cream

500g (1lb) ribbon noodles

METHOD
Sauté onions and celery in the butter for a few minutes. Stir in chopped tomatoes, tomato paste, crumbled stock cube and the basil. Add a little water if necessary and simmer to a rich thick sauce.

Taste for seasoning and add salt and pepper if necessary. Gently heat the cheese and cream together, mix with the hot, drained noodles. Serve in deep plates with the tomato sauce spooned on the top.

PASTA WITH HERBS
Serves 4 Appetisers

INGREDIENTS
8-10 lasagne sheets

1 tablespoon vegetable oil

½ cup chopped parsley

¼ cup chopped fresh basil

⅓ cup water

2 tablespoons butter

½ cup grated Parmesan cheese

METHOD
Cook lasagne sheets in boiling salted water with the oil until tender.

Mix parsley and basil together. Heat water, stir in butter until melted and add parsley and basil.

Drain lasagne, place on individual plates, sprinkle with Parmesan and pour over the herb sauce.

Opposite page: Noodles with Fresh Tomato Sauce, recipe above.

JAMBALAYA
Serves 4-5

INGREDIENTS
1 x 425g can whole
  peeled tomatoes,
  chopped, and their
  liquid
Chicken stock or water
3 tablespoons butter
  or oil
1 large onion, finely
  chopped
1 clove of garlic, crushed
1 medium green
  capsicum, diced
2 cups long grain rice
Salt
Freshly ground black
  pepper
1 tablespoon chopped
  parsley
4 slices of cooked ham,
  diced
250g (8oz) prawns,
  peeled and deveined
2 breasts of cooked
  chicken, diced
Tabasco
Chopped parsley

METHOD
Measure the tomatoes and their liquid and add enough
stock to make 3 cups. Heat gently until boiling. Heat the
butter or oil in a large pan, add the onion, garlic, and
capsicum, and fry gently for 1–2 minutes. Add the rice and
stir over low heat for 2–3 minutes. Mix in salt and black
pepper to taste, the parsley, and the ham. Add the boiling
tomato mixture, cover tightly, and cook over low heat for
20 minutes, or until the rice is tender and liquid has been
absorbed, adding a little more stock if necessary.

Scatter the prawns and chicken over the top, replace the
lid, and return to very low heat until the prawns are
heated through. Sprinkle with Tabasco and chopped parsley,
and serve.

NOODLES WITH ROQUEFORT
Serves 4 entrées

INGREDIENTS
500g (1lb) broccoli
2 tablespoons butter
2 cloves garlic, finely
  chopped
500g (1lb) ribbon
  noodles, cooked
90g (3oz) Roquefort

METHOD
Divide broccoli into small heads and cook in boiling salted
water until still crisp. Melt butter, add garlic and cook very
gently until softened, but not brown. Toss the hot cooked
noodles with the garlic butter and place on individual
serving plates together with the drained broccoli. Crumble
the Roquefort over the top.

KEDGEREE
Serves 5

INGREDIENTS
½ cup long grain rice
500g (1lb) smoked
  cod or haddock
1 egg
2 tablespoons cream
3 tablespoons butter
2 hard-boiled eggs,
  roughly chopped
2 teaspoons curry
  powder
1 tablespoon chopped
  parsley

METHOD
Cook the rice in boiling salted water for about 12 minutes; drain thoroughly.

Poach the fish in water until tender; drain, remove skin and bones, and flake.

Beat the egg with the cream. Melt the butter in a large saucepan. Stir in the rice, fish, chopped eggs, and the curry powder. Stir, using a fork, until very hot. Remove from the heat, add the egg and cream, and mix well. Serve sprinkled with the chopped parsley.

PASTA WITH MOZZARELLA
Serves 4

INGREDIENTS
8 zucchini
4 cloves garlic, thinly
  sliced
60g (2oz) butter
Salt to taste
Freshly ground pepper
500g (1lb) spaghetti,
  cooked
185g (6oz) mozarella,
  sliced thinly

METHOD
Cut zucchini lengthwise into thin julienne strips. Cook with the garlic in the butter for a few minutes.

Drain the hot cooked spaghetti and toss with the zucchini mixture. Season with salt and pepper. Place in serving bowls, add the cheese and let it soften. Serve with salad.

tablespoons butter 1/2 cup plain flour 1/2 teaspoon salt 2 cups milk 4
og (3oz) Swiss cheese, shredded Swiss cheese sauce: 90g (3oz) butter 1
heese, shredded method Lightly grease a 37 x 25 x 2 cm (15 x 10 x 1 i
our. Melt the butter in a saucepan. Stir in the flour and salt and coo
ilk. Return to the heat and cook, stirring constantly, until very thick.
owly beat the sauce mixture into the yolks until blended. Fold in the
inutes, or until the top is golden and springs back when touched light
ie hot broccoli and three-quarters of the cheese on top; pour over h
atter. Pour the remaining sauce over and sprinkle with the rest of th
saucepan. Add the flour, salt and pepper. Stir constantly over low

Vegetables
and salads

parated 1 x 238g packet of frozen broccoli cooked, drained and choppe
lain flour 1/2 teaspoon salt Pinch of pepper 3 cups milk 90g (3oz) Swis
roll tin; line with greaseproof paper, grease the paper, and dust wit
ew minutes, stirring constantly. Remove from the heat and stir in th
minute. Beat the egg whites until stiff. Beat the egg yolks until cream
egg whites. Pour into the prepared tin. Bake in a moderate oven for 4
he fingertip. Carefully turn out of the tin and peel off the paper. Spoo
heese sauce. Roll up, Swiss-roll fashion. Transfer the roll to a servin
e. Cut into thick slices to serve. Swiss cheese sauce: Melt the butter
radually add the milk and continue cooking, stirring until the sauc

WALNUT AVOCADO SALAD
Serves 4

INGREDIENTS
Assorted lettuce leaves
3-4 small ripe avocados
½ cup walnut pieces
2 teaspoons white wine
  vinegar
1 teaspoon French
  mustard
Salt and pepper to taste
2 tablespoons walnut oil
½ cup raisins

METHOD
Arrange lettuce leaves on individual serving plates. Peel avocados and cut into slices.

Sprinkle over the walnuts.

Beat together vinegar, mustard, salt and pepper. Add oil a drop at a time, beating continuously so that the dressing is thick. Add raisins, pour over avocado and serve.

CRUNCHY CUCUMBER SALAD
Serves 4

INGREDIENTS
1 large green cucumber
1 cup chopped shallots
1 tablespoon chopped
  fresh mint
2 teaspoons chopped
  fresh basil
¼ cup sultanas
½ cup chopped walnuts
1 cup natural yoghurt
½ teaspoon salt

METHOD
Slice or chop cucumber into pieces and combine with all other ingredients.

Chill thoroughly, place in salad bowl and serve.

MUSHROOMS À LA GREQUE
Serves 4

INGREDIENTS

500g (1lb) small
  mushrooms, wiped
  with a damp cloth
1 tablespoon lemon juice
1 clove of garlic, crushed
1 tablespoon chopped
  parsley
2 medium tomatoes,
  peeled and chopped
1 tablespoon tomato
  paste
½ cup water
Pinch of dried oregano
Salt
Freshly ground black
  pepper
½ cup thinly sliced celery
1 bay leaf
¼ cup olive oil

METHOD

Trim the stems off the mushrooms. Put the lemon juice in a saucepan with the garlic, parsley, tomatoes, tomato paste, and water. Bring to the boil, stirring. Add the mushrooms, oregano, salt and black pepper to taste, the celery, bay leaf, and olive oil. Cover and simmer for 8-10 minutes. Cool and then chill in the refrigerator.

RATATOUILLE
Serves 4

INGREDIENTS
1 small eggplant
Salt to taste
2-3 tablespoons olive oil
500g (1lb) zucchini,
  sliced
2 onions, sliced
1 red capsicum, sliced
500g (1lb) tomatoes,
  chopped
1 clove garlic, crushed
2 tablespoons chopped
  parsley
Salt and freshly ground
  black pepper

METHOD
Cut eggplant into slices. Place in a colander. Sprinkle with salt and leave one hour.

Rinse and pat dry.

Heat oil in a heavy frypan. Add eggplant, sliced zucchini, onions and capsicum and cook a few minutes. Add tomatoes, garlic, parsley, salt and pepper to taste. Cover with a tight-fitting lid and cook a little longer until vegetables are tender but crisp.

Do not overcook. Serve by itself or with pasta dishes.

STUFFED VEGETABLES
Serves 3-6

INGREDIENTS
3 large well shaped
    capsicums
1 tablespoon butter
1 medium onion, finely
    chopped
1 clove garlic, crushed
¼ teaspoon dried basil
1 tablespoon tomato
    paste
¼ cup cream
1 egg, beaten
2 tablespoons wheatgerm
Salt and pepper
Pinch of sugar
1 x 250g (8oz) can
    3-bean mix, drained
½ cup small shell
    macaroni, cooked and
    drained
½ cup grated Parmesan
    cheese

METHOD
Cut the capsicums in halves lengthwise, remove seeds and
core and blanch in boiling water 2 minutes. Refresh under
cold running water and drain.

Melt the butter in a small saucepan and fry the onion,
garlic and basil until onion is transparent. Remove from
heat and mix in the tomato paste, cream, egg, wheatgerm,
salt, pepper and sugar. Stir in the beans and shell macaroni.
Spoon into the capsicums, sprinkle with cheese and bake in
a moderate oven 15-20 minutes or until capsicums
are tender.

Zucchini, eggplant and tomatoes may be filled and baked
in the same way, but eggplant and tomatoes do not need
blanching.

MELON SALAD
Serves 4-5

INGREDIENTS
½ honeydew melon,
    peeled and diced
1 cup seedless green
    grapes
1 cup diced pineapple
2 peaches, peeled and
    diced
2 apples, peeled and
    diced
1 cup sliced celery
Shredded lettuce

METHOD
Combine melon, grapes, pineapple, peaches, apples and
celery. Place half in a salad bowl. Add a layer of shredded
lettuce. Cover with remaining fruit mixture.

Chill thoroughly before serving and serve with salad
dressing   either a little poured over top or separately.

*Pumpkin Scone Wedge,
recipe page 249 and
Stuffed Vegetables, recipe
page 226, are two
appetising examples*

BROCCOLI ROULADE
Serves 6

INGREDIENTS
4 tablespoons butter
½ cup plain flour
½ teaspoon salt
2 cups milk
4 eggs, separated
1 x 238g packet of
    frozen broccoli
    cooked, drained and
    chopped
90g (3oz) Swiss
    cheese, shredded

Swiss cheese sauce:
90g (3oz) butter
½ cup plain flour
½ teaspoon salt
Pinch of pepper
3 cups milk
90g (3oz) Swiss
    cheese, shredded

METHOD
Lightly grease a 37 x 25 x 2 cm (15 x 10 x 1 in) Swiss roll tin; line with greaseproof paper, grease the paper, and dust with flour. Melt the butter in a saucepan. Stir in the flour and salt and cook for a few minutes, stirring constantly. Remove from the heat and stir in the milk. Return to the heat and cook, stirring constantly, until very thick.

Boil for 1 minute. Beat the egg whites until stiff. Beat the egg yolks until creamy. Slowly beat the sauce mixture into the yolks until blended. Fold in the beaten egg whites. Pour into the prepared tin. Bake in a moderate oven for 45 minutes, or until the top is golden and springs back when touched lightly with the fingertip. Carefully turn out of the tin and peel off the paper.

Spoon the hot broccoli and three-quarters of the cheese on top; pour over half the cheese sauce. Roll up, Swiss-roll fashion. Transfer the roll to a serving platter. Pour the remaining sauce over and sprinkle with the rest of the cheese.

Cut into thick slices to serve.

Swiss cheese sauce: Melt the butter in a saucepan. Add the flour, salt and pepper. Stir constantly over low heat. Gradually add the milk and continue cooking, stirring until the sauce thickens. Boil for 1 minute and then stir in the cheese.

Stir until cheese has melted.

The health food movement which swept into Australia during the early 20th century has settled into our national cuisine. The fact that fresh, wholesome often purely vegetarian food can be as delicious as any other if it is tastefully prepared has captured the imagination of many people who base their diet on fruit, vegetables, pulses and grains.

SWEET POTATO PURÉE
Serves 6

INGREDIENTS
5 large sweet potatoes,
    coarsely chopped
3 Granny Smith apples,
    peeled, cored, chopped
½ cup evaporated milk,
    heated
2 tablespoons melted
    butter
Pinch of nutmeg
    (optional)
Salt and pepper

METHOD
Cook the potatoes in boiling salted water until tender; drain thoroughly. Cook the apples gently in ½ cup water until tender; drain well. Purée the potatoes and apples in a blender, then transfer to a bowl. Add the hot evaporated milk, the melted butter and nutmeg, seasoning with salt and pepper to taste. Whisk until smooth, then pile into a warmed serving bowl. This is good with roast veal, lamb, pork or chicken, and with pork chops.

LUNCHEON BOUQUET
Serves 4

INGREDIENTS

125g (4oz) mushrooms
1 tablespoon lemon juice
Endive or lettuce of
    your choice
8 canned asparagus
    spears
1 ripe avocado, sliced
1 cup sliced celery
2 hard-boiled eggs,
    quartered
½ cup thinly sliced
    cucumber
1 small Spanish onion,
    sliced thinly
½ cup pecans
2 cups cooked brown
    rice, chilled
1 punnet cherry
    tomatoes

Horseradish dressing:
¼ cup whole egg
    mayonnaise
3 tablespoons cream
1 teaspoon horseradish
    cream

METHOD

Slice mushrooms and sprinkle with the lemon juice.
Arrange endive on 4 salad plates with asparagus spears and
sliced avocado. Combine celery, hard-boiled eggs,
cucumber, onion, pecans, rice, tomatoes and mushrooms.
Pile onto salad plates chill thoroughly. Combine Dressing
ingredients and pour over salad just before serving.
    Serve with crusty bread.

x 100g block cooking chocolate 125g (4oz) butter 2 cups brown sugar 1 t
carbonate of soda 3/4 cup sour cream 1/2 cup boiling water Butt
iblespoons sherry or cherry brandy 1/2 cup chopped glacé cherries (
ater. Beat together butter, sugar and vanilla essence until creamy
nocolate. Mix in sifted dry ingredients alternately with sour cream a
iper-lined 20 cm (8 in) sandwich cake tins and bake in a moderate ou
minutes before removing cake tins. These cakes are soft and delicate
id join the 3 layers together. Cover top and sides with the remainde

Desserts & cakes

n vanilla essence 3 eggs 2 cups self-raising flour Pinch salt 1/2 teaspo
m filling and frosting: 250g (8oz) butter 4 cups icing sugar, sifted
walnuts Whole maraschino cherries method Melt chocolate over ho
ggs one at a time and beat well after each addition. Beat in melte
g water and beat until smooth. Divide evenly into 3 greased and bas
oximately 30 minutes until cooked. Invert onto cake coolers and leau
dle carefully. Mix the glacé cherries into a quarter of the butter crea
ving some for piping on the top. Spread smoothly and press choppe

PAVLOVA CROWN

INGREDIENTS
6 egg whites
1¾ cups caster sugar
2 teaspoons cornflour
1 teaspoon vinegar
1 teaspoon vanilla
　　essence
1½ cups cream, whipped
1 tablespoon icing
　　sugar, sifted
Pulp 3-4 passionfruit
Strawberries
Mulberries

METHOD
Beat egg whites until stiff peaks form. Add sugar gradually, beating on high speed on electric mixer until thick and glossy. Fold in cornflour, vinegar and vanilla essence.

Spread three-quarters of the mixture onto an oven tray lined with baking paper and shape into an oblong. Spoon the remaining meringue mixture into small mounds onto baking paper lined oven trays.

Bake both in a slow oven about 1 hour until lightly coloured and crisp.

Remove from oven and cool.

Mix cream and icing sugar together and spread over the oblong base. Press the small meringues into the cream around the edge.

Cover cream with passionfruit and decorate with strawberries and mulberries.

MANGO JELLY
Serves 4-5

INGREDIENTS
1 large ripe mango
2 tablespoons sherry
¼ cup orange juice
1 tablespoon lemon juice
¼ cup icing sugar, sifted
3 teaspoons gelatine
¾ cup thickened cream,
　　whipped
Papaw, melon wedges,
　　kiwi fruit and
　　passionfruit, for
　　decoration

METHOD
Peel mango, cut flesh from stone and pulverise in a processor. Tip into a basin and stir in sherry, orange and lemon juice, and icing sugar.

Soften gelatine in a little cold water and stir over hot water until dissolved. Cool.

Fold into mango mixture together with whipped cream.

Pour into a wet or lightly oiled 4-cup mould and chill until set. Unmould onto a serving platter and surround with papaw and melon wedges, sliced kiwi fruit and passionfruit.

Some cynics have said that the pavlova was originally created in New Zealand. Nevertheless, this delectable meringue dessert traditionally filled with whipped cream and fruit, has settled into the Australian cuisine as one of its most popular dishes. The creamy filling can be flavoured with liqueur, vanilla, chocolate or lemon, combined with glacé, canned or fresh fruits. This version, called Pavlova Crown, recipe page 212, is decorated with a ring of small meringues and garnished with passionfruit and berries.

Opposite page: Mango Jelly, recipe above. Following page: Pavlova Crown with Passionfruit and Berries.

SOLDIER'S CHRISTMAS CAKE

INGREDIENTS
250g (8oz) seeded
  raisins, chopped
250g (8oz) sultanas
250g (8oz) currants
125g (4oz) glacé
  cherries, chopped
125g (4oz) chopped
  mixed peel
125g (4oz) blanched
  almonds, chopped
⅔ cup brandy or orange
  juice
2 cups plain flour
½ cup self-raising flour
Pinch of salt
½ teaspoon nutmeg
½ teaspoon cinnamon
1 teaspoon mixed spice
250g (8oz) butter
1½ cups brown sugar
2 tablespoons dark jam
  or marmalade
4 eggs

METHOD
Mix the seeded raisins with the sultanas, currants, cherries, mixed peel, and almonds.

Sprinkle with the brandy or orange juice.

Sift the flours with the salt and spices. Beat the butter and brown sugar until light and fluffy. Add the jam and beat again. Add the eggs, one at a time, beating well after each addition.

Fold in the fruit and flour mixtures alternately. Mix thoroughly. Spoon into a deep 20cm (8in) round cake tin, lined with two layers each of aluminium foil and grease-proof paper. Bake in a moderate oven for 30 minutes. Reduce heat to moderately slow and cook 2½ - 3 hours. Test with a fine skewer before removing from oven.

MOCHA ICE-CREAM
Serves 4

INGREDIENTS
1 x 500ml carton
  vanilla custard
1 x 300ml container
  thickened cream
1 teaspoon instant coffee
1 teaspoon gelatine,
  softened in a little
  cold water
1 cup grated chocolate
Coffee or chocolate beans
Chocolate liqueur

METHOD
Mix custard and cream together. Place instant coffee and softened gelatine in a small saucepan and stir over a low heat until dissolved. Cool, then stir into cream with grated chocolate.

Freeze quickly. Spoon into sweet dishes, top with beans and pour over liqueur to taste.

CHOCOLATE ICE-CREAM CAKE
Serves 4

INGREDIENTS
4 slices sponge or
    buttercake
4 scoops vanilla ice-
    cream

Chocolate fudge sauce:
1 x 100g block dark
    chocolate
¾ cup cream or
    evaporated milk
1 egg
½ cup lightly filled
    brown sugar
1 teaspoon vanilla
essence

METHOD
Place cake slices on serving plate and top with generous
scoops of ice-cream.

Spoon over chocolate sauce and serve. For a variation,
use the chocolate sauce while hot, otherwise chill first, then
spoon over ice-cream.

Chocolate Fudge Sauce: Melt chocolate gently in a
double saucepan. Beat cream, egg and sugar together and
gradually stir into melted chocolate.

Cook over simmering water for 20 minutes, stirring all
the time until thickened. Stir in vaniilla essence. Cool.
Keeps well in refrigerator for several days. If mixture
thickens too much during storage, thin down before using
with a little cream or hot water.

NUTTY ANZAC BISCUITS
Makes 30-40

INGREDIENTS
1 cup plain flour
1 cup rolled oats
¼ cup sugar
¼ cup desiccated coconut
½ cup chopped peanuts
2 tablespoons golden
    syrup
125g (4oz) butter
1 teaspoon bicarbonate
    of soda
3 tablespoons boiling
    water

METHOD
Mix the flour, oats, sugar, coconut and peanuts together.
Melt the syrup and butter over a gentle heat. Dissolve the
bicarbonate of soda in the boiling water, stir in the syrup
mixture, and pour over the dry ingredients, stirring until
well mixed.

Put heaped teaspoons of the mixture, about 5 cm (2 in)
apart to allow for spreading, on greased oven trays. Bake in
a moderately slow oven for about 20 minutes. Remove
from oven and leave on the trays a few minutes, then lift off
with a spatula.

*Following pages: Anzac
Biscuits (Nutty Anzac
Biscuits), recipe this page,
and Soldier's Christmas
Cake, recipe page 216
were baked by loving
wives and mothers to send
in food parcels to
Australian soldiers fighting
overseas in the Great War
of 1914-1918.*

SORBETS WITH MELON SAUCE
Serves 4-5

KIWI SORBET

INGREDIENTS
6 ripe kiwi fruit
2 tablespoons lemon
  juice
2 tablespoons icing
  sugar, sifted

METHOD
Peel kiwi fruit and whizz in a blender until smooth. Stir in lemon juice and icing sugar.

Pour into a freezer-proof bowl and place in freezer. Beat every 15-20 minutes until frozen.

It should be smooth and fluffy.

RASPBERRY SORBET

INGREDIENTS
375g (12oz) fresh or
  frozen raspberries
¼ cup icing sugar, sifted

METHOD
Pulverise berries in a blender and strain through a fine strainer to remove all seeds.
Stir in icing sugar.
Pour into a freezer-proof bowl and place in freezer. Beat every 15-20 minutes until frozen.

PINEAPPLE SORBET

INGREDIENTS
1 x 450g can crushed
  pineapple, drained
1 tablespoon lemon
  juice
1 egg white

METHOD
Place pineapple in a food processor or blender and whizz until smooth. Stir in lemon juice and unbeaten egg white.

Pour into a freezer-proof bowl and place in freezer. Beat every 15-20 minutes until frozen.

MELON SAUCE

INGREDIENTS
4 cups watermelon
  cubes

METHOD
Take care to remove all seeds from melon. Pulverise in a blender until smooth.

Pour onto individual plates and top with a spoonful of each of the sorbets.

May be served with melon wedges, sliced kiwi fruit, grapes or strawberries dipped in chocolate, tiny cakes or wafer biscuits

Opposite page:
Sorbets with Melon
Sauce, recipes above.

CREAM PUFFS ROYALE
Makes 20-24

INGREDIENTS
1 cup water
125g (4oz) butter
1 teaspoon sugar
Pinch salt
1 cup plain flour
4 eggs
Whipped, sweetened
  cream
Icing sugar

METHOD
Place water, butter, sugar and salt in a saucepan and heat until butter melts and liquid is boiling.

Add sifted flour all at once to boiling liquid and stir vigorously with a wooden spoon until mixture comes away from the sides of the saucepan.

Remove from heat and allow to cool for a few minutes. Beat in eggs one at a time until smooth and shiny.

Spoon or pipe mounds onto baking sheets lined with baking paper and cook in a hot oven 20 minutes. Reduce heat to moderately-hot and bake another 10-15 minutes until puffs are golden brown and crisp to touch. Make a small slit in the sides of each puff to allow the steam to escape and return to a warm oven to dry the centres. Cool on wire racks.

Cut tops off puffs and pipe or spoon in the sweetened whipped cream. Replace tops and sieve icing sugar over just before serving.

DUTCH HONEY CAKE

INGREDIENTS
2 cups plain flour
½ teaspoon bicarbonate
  of soda
1 teaspoon cinnamon
1 teaspoon ground
  cardamom
1 teaspoon ground
  ginger
½ teaspoon ground
  cloves
3 eggs
½ cup vegetable oil
¾ cup honey
¾ cup lightly filled dark
  brown sugar

Lemond icing: (recipe follows)
Preserved ginger, sliced

METHOD
Sift dry ingredients into large bowl of electric mixer. Add all remaining ingredients and beat 5 minutes.

Pour into a greased 20 cm (8 in) ring cake tin. Bake in a moderate oven until cooked, about 50 minutes. Cool and ice with thin lemon icing and decorate with sliced preserved ginger.

Lemon Icing: Place 1 cup sifted icing sugar into a small saucepan, add 1 teaspoon copha and enough lemon juice to mix to a pouring consistency. Stir over a low heat until copha has melted. Pour over cake and spread to edges.

STRAWBERRIES ARABIA
Serves 2

INGREDIENTS
1 punnet strawberries
1 orange
¼ cup orange brandy
   liqueur

METHOD
Slice strawberries and place in a serving bowl. Peel rind from orange very thinly with a vegetable peeler and cut into thin strips. Add to strawberries together with the strained orange juice.

Pour over the liqueur, cover and chill 2-3 hours. Delicious with pouring cream or ice-cream.

BLACK FOREST CAKE

INGREDIENTS
1 x 100g block
   cooking chocolate
125g (4oz) butter
2 cups brown sugar
1 teaspoon vanilla
   essence
3 eggs
2 cups self-raising flour
Pinch salt
½ teaspoon bicarbonate
   of soda
¾ cup sour cream
½ cup boiling water

*Butter Cream filling and
frosting:*
250g (8oz) butter
4 cups icing sugar, sifted
2 tablespoons sherry or
   cherry brandy
½ cup chopped glacé
   cherries
Chopped walnuts
Whole maraschino
   cherries

METHOD
Melt chocolate over hot water. Beat together butter, sugar and vanilla essence until creamy. Add eggs one at a time and beat well after each addition. Beat in melted chocolate. Mix in sifted dry ingredients alternately with sour cream and boiling water and beat until smooth.

Divide evenly into 3 greased and base paper-lined 20 cm (8 in) sandwich cake tins and bake in a moderate oven approximately 30 minutes until cooked. Invert onto cake coolers and leave 5 minutes before removing cake tins. These cakes are soft and delicate so handle carefully.

Mix the glacé cherries into a quarter of the butter cream and join the 3 layers together.

Cover top and sides with the remainder, reserving some for piping on the top. Spread smoothly and press chopped walnuts around the outside.

Decorate top by piping swirls of the butter cream around edge and adding a few whole maraschino cherries.

Butter cream filling and frosting: Beat butter until soft and pale. Gradually add icing sugar and sherry or liqueur, beating until smooth and creamy.

NOTE: Morello sour cherries may be used in place of glacé cherries if desired.

The following cakes are legacies from Holland and Germany introduced by the proprietors of European cake shops in the 30's and 40's. The Australian honeybee is also a newcomer, its ancestors coming from Britain in 1822 on the sailing ship Isabella. Following pages: Dutch Honey Cake, left, recipe page 222, and Black Forest Cake, right, recipe above.

FRENCH APPLE TART
Serves 6-8

INGREDIENTS
1 x 375 g packet frozen
puff pastry, thawed
4 cooking apples, peeled
and sliced thinly
½ cup apricot jam
1 tablespoon white wine
or water

METHOD
Roll out pastry into a circle and line a shallow 28 cm (11
in) pie plate or pizza tray.

Cover with apple slices, overlapping and placed close
together.

Heat jam and wine together and carefully brush over
apple slices. Bake in a hot oven 25-30 minutes, brushing
now and again with remaining jam. At the end of cooking
time, if desired, place under a hot grill to give a glazed
look. Serve warm.

FEDERATION CHARLOTTE
Serves 5-6

INGREDIENTS
16-20 sponge fingers,
sides and ends
trimmed
1 egg white
1 x 600 ml container
thickened cream
2 teaspoons icing sugar
1 tablespoon Grand
Marnier or other
liqueur
5 teaspoons gelatine
¼ cup orange juice
Red jelly

METHOD
Line a 5-cup mould with oiled greaseproof paper, oiled side
down, cut to fit. Arrange sponge fingers evenly around side
of mould, packed closely together and long enough to reach
top of tin evenly. Brush joins with a little white of egg to
seal. Line bottom of mould with sponge fingers, cut in
triangles to fit. Whip the cream until thick, add icing sugar
and liqueur.

Dissolve the gelatine in the orange juice, cool and stir
slowly into the cream, stirring all the time. When mixture
begins to thicken pour into the mould. Refrigerate until
set. Turn out onto a paper doily on a glass or silver dish,
preferably stemmed. Decorate with fresh berries, chopped
red jelly and a bow-tied ribbon sash.

*Opposite page:
French Apple Tart, recipe
above.
Following pages: Cream
Puffs Royale, recipe page
222; Federation
Charlotte, recipe above.*

PUMPKIN SCONE WEDGE
Makes 8 wedges

INGREDIENTS
2 tablespoons butter
2 tablespoons sugar
1 cup mashed, well-
    drained, cooked
    pumpkin
1 egg
2 cups self-raising flour
Pinch salt
⅓ cup sultanas
Milk for glazing

METHOD
Beat together butter and sugar until creamy, mix in the pumpkin and egg.

Sift the flour and salt and mix in, together with the sultanas.

Knead lightly on a floured surface. Pat into a 20 cm (8 in) round and place on a lightly greased oven tray. Cut into 8 sections almost to the bottom so that they can be pulled apart when baked. Brush with milk and bake in a hot oven for 20-25 minutes until cooked.

MILK CHOCOLATE MOUSSE
Serves 4

INGREDIENTS
125 g (4 oz) milk
    chocolate
3 eggs, separated
1 x 300 ml container
    thickened cream
Toasted almond slivers
Grated chocolate

METHOD
Melt chocolate gently in a double saucepan. Remove from heat and beat in egg yolks one at a time, beating vigorously.

Beat egg whites until stiff and then whip the cream until thick. Fold chocolate into egg whites and then carefully fold in half the whipped cream.

Alternate layers of chocolate mixture and whipped cream into 4 parfait glasss. Finish with cream on top and chill. Just before serving top with toasted slivered almonds and a little grated chocolate.

APPLE CHEESCAKE
Serves 6 8

INGREDIENTS
¾ cup plain flour
60g (2oz) butter, softened
2 teaspoons water
Red jam
2 apples, peeled, cored and sliced
¼ cup sultanas
1 cup cottage cheese, sieved
½ cup plain flour
½ cup sugar
3 eggs
Grated rind 1 lemon
1 tablespoon lemon juice
½ cup cream, whipped

METHOD
Mix flour, butter and water together into a dough. Press evenly onto base of a greased 23 cm (9 in) springform tin. Spread with jam. Cover with apple slices and half the sultanas.

Beat together the cottage cheese, flour, sugar, eggs, lemon rind, juice and the remaining sultanas. Fold in whipped cream and pour over the apples.

Bake in a hot oven 25 minutes until set and top is lightly brown. Sift icing sugar over top and serve warm.

Opposite page:
Apple Cheesecake, recipe above.

Index

Art captions

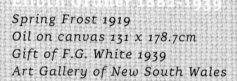

Page 17

Page 27

Elioth Gruner 1882-1939

Spring Frost 1919
Oil on canvas 131 x 178.7cm
Gift of F.G. White 1939
Art Gallery of New South Wales

This small homestead, built on a free land grant of 30 acres given to convict James Ruse in 1789, was one of the first properties established around Sydney and Parramatta.

It was here that vegetables and fruit were cultivated for the colony, and strawberries were grown from offshoots of a single root that Governor Phillip had brought with him. In 1794 the first plough was introduced, and agriculture began.

Then citrus fruits and many varieties of apples and pears from Tasmania and Victoria became available, enabling industrious housewives to make jams and preserves. Our delicious Apple-Marmalade pie, page 89, could well have been a typical dish of the time.

Rupert Bunny 1864-1947

Worked in Europe 1884-1933.
Shrimp Fishers at Saint-Georges (Pêcheurs de crevettes à Saint-Georges) c.1910
Oil on canvas 120.7 x 161.9cm
Felton Bequest 1946
National Gallery of Victoria, Melbourne

Rambles by the sea were favourite family outings in the early days of Australia, just as they still are today. This group of amateur fishers, absorbed by the task of trying to catch some shrimps or small prawns, would probably have been disappointed, but they present a charming picture just the same. Prawns have always been regarded as a delicacy in Australia, despite their abundance. Fresh prawns were sold in the streets of Sydney in the 1850s for sixpence a pint. Since then, they have gradually become an expensive luxury, only to be eaten on special occasions. Prawn cocktails have been popular first courses for decades, and buckets of prawns are often served at parties and barbecues, or on the peculiarly Australian "prawn night" celebrations in pubs.

Page 39

Page 51

Graham Lupp 1983

Chickens
Watercolour 29 x 50 cm
Private Collection

The poor inhabitants of this tumbledown little house would probably have lived on mutton, bread and tea, the staple diet of early Australian settlers. During the Depression, baked or stewed rabbit was a cheap sustaining meal. A dish of chicken varied the monotony, but only on special occasions such as Sundays, Easter and Christmas. Elaborately sauced frenchified poultry dishes were fashionable restaurant and banquet fare for moneyed people. Among the working classes, English style roast chicken with stuffing, bread sauce and roast vegetables became a popular Sunday midday dinner which gradually declined as supermarket battery chickens became cheap and plentiful.

Sali Herman b. 1898

Near the Docks 1949
Oil on canvas 50.7 x 96.8cm
purchased 1949
Art Gallery of New South Wales

Dishes such as Irish stew and cooked pig's trotters would probably have been popular among the original residents of these simple workmen's cottages and terrace houses in old Sydney Town. Streets such as this one proliferated as immigrants poured into Australia in the 19th century looking for work and possible wealth. The well-to-do lived in larger houses with gardens and enjoyed a basically British diet from the better cuts of meat. Our recipe for Gentleman's Breakfast on page 80 could have been prepared in the kitchens of a merchant or businessman's house or club, maybe a lodging house or hotel, as a variation on the adopted porridge, lamb chop, bacon and eggs, toast and marmalade breakfast fare of England.

Page 71

Page 123

Hugh Ramsay 1877-1906

The Sisters, 1904
Oil on canvas on hardboard 125.7 x 144.8cm
purchased 1921
Art Gallery of New South Wales

The artist's sisters sitting so petulantly in
their satin and tulle gowns in Hugh
Ramsay's painting above are obviously well-
to-do turn-of-the-century Australians.
Have they just returned from a ball? Are
they going to one of the elaborate banquets
so popular at the time? Perhaps they are
waiting for their carriage to take them to
the opera or the theatre. In any case they
would undoubtedly indulge in many
sumptuous meals of rich party food ending
with the sweet French or English puddings
which were so popular at the time.

John Skinner Prout 1806-1876

(Bush landscape with waterfall and an
aborigine stalking native animals, New
South Wales, 1860's)
Oil on canvas 70.5 x 91.4cm
Purchased under the terms of the Florence
Turner Blake bequest 1976
Art Gallery of New South Wales

Page 87

William Ford c.1820-c.1886

Born Great Britain (c.1820), arrived in
Australia (c.1870), died (c.1886)
At the Hanging Rock 1875
Oil on canvas 79.2 x 117.5cm
purchased 1950
National Gallery of Victoria, Melbourne

Australians have always loved picnics. Eating
outdoors was borne of necessity in the
earliest days of the colony when shelter was
scarce and dining rooms nonexistent. But the
taste for eating outside lingered, developed
and then flourished long after there was
housing for all, however grand or humble.

Would the picnickers here have ever
guessed that their day's outing would be
celebrated a hundred years later as the title
of a famous Australian film adapted from
the novel "Picnic at Hanging Rock" ? They
would have travelled to the high country
outside Melbourne, Victoria, by coach,
wagonette or train and then reached the
strange bushland with its tall trees on Foot.
The food brought with them was most likely
modelled on the picnic provisions
popularised in the 1860s by Mrs Beaton
and her book. Pies, fruit cakes and a
huge selection of cold foods in
staggering proportions were deemed
correct fare for such an occasion
whether it be in England, India or any
of the British colonies.

Page 135

David Strachan 1919-1970
Fish, 1953
Oil on wood 37.8 x 40.7cm
purchased 1954
Art Gallery of New South Wales
© estate of the artist

Page 151

Ena Joyce
After Lunch 1982
Gouache 37.5 x 55cm
Bathurst Regional Art Gallery

**Ethel Spowers
Australia 1890-1947**

*Bank Holiday 1935
Colour linocut 24.6 x 25.0cm
Felton Bequest 1937
National Gallery of Victoria, Melbourne*

The average Australian enjoys many long
weekends throughout the year. National,
memorial, commercial and religious days are
often tacked on to weekends to shorten
numerous working weeks. Any opportunity
to escape from the routine of work to the
beach or the bush is welcomed, often with
blissful disregard for the original reason for
the holiday.

The family-style picnic portrayed in this
linocut shows a group of people temporarily
free from the cares of life as they were at
the time; the still difficult period of
economic recovery after the Depression.
They are obviously relaxed and happy and
preparing to enjoy an alfresco meal which
seems to consist of billy tea, sandwiches,
cakes, beer and a pineapple.

Elayne Russell

*Figs and Capsicums 1983
Pastel on paper 65.5 x 99.5cm
Bathurst Regional Art Gallery*

Page 201

Page 212

Jean Bellette
Still Life with Wooden Bowl, [date unknown]
Oil on hardboard 54.6 x 81.3cm
purchased 1954
Art Gallery of New South Wales
© AGNSW

Grace Cossington-Smith 1892-1984
The Lacquer Room, 1935-1936
Oil on paperboard on plywood 74 x 90.8cm
purchased 1967
Art Gallery of New South Wales
© AGNSW

In the 1930s eating in restaurants was usually out of the question. For the hard-up, even a simple meal in a cheap restaurant was an extravagance; probably steak and eggs or a Chinese meal were the ultimate weekend treat. Lunchtime sandwiches were usually replaced by a light lunchtime snack in a tearoom or coffee shop where they mingled with commercial travellers or tired housewives on shopping trips to the city.

The bare tables and sparse Art Deco trim of the cafe in this painting accurately illustrate the mood of the time. This feeling is further emphasised by the impersonal attitudes of the waitresses and the lonely almost desperate expressions on the faces of the customers.

Bibliography

Old Days: Old Ways by Mary Gilmore
Sirius Books,
Angus & Robertson Ltd.
First published in June, 1934
First published by Sirius in 1963

Our Home in Australia
A Description of Cottage
Life in 1860 by Joseph Elliott
The Flannel Flower Press,
Sydney, 1984

One Continuous Picnic
A History of Eating in Australia
by Michael Symons
Penguin Books, 1984

Colonial Food & Drink 1788–1901
Published by the Historic Houses
Trust of New South Wales in
conjunction with an exhibition
at Elizabeth Bay House,
December 1985 – May 1986

*Australia As Once We Were by
John Ritchie*
William Heinemann Australia
Pty. Ltd. 1975

*Advice to a Young Lady in the Colonies
being a letter sent from Mrs. E of
England to Maria Macarthur in the
Colony of New South Wales in 1812*
Greenhouse Publications
Pty. Ltd., 1979

The Shearers by Patsy Adam-Smith
Nelson, 1982

*Beeton's Book of Household
Management*
Originally published in London
by S.O. Beeton, 1861
Reproduced by Jonathan Cape
Limited, London, 1968

MEASUREMENTS

Recipe measurements in this book are given in
metric units with imperial units in brackets.
Use either metric
or imperial measurements, but never mix
them. Australian standard metric measuring
spoons and cups are used in the recipes in
this book. Eggs are 55 g size.
1 Australian metric cup is 250 ml.
1 Australian metric tablespoon is 20 ml.
1 Australian metric teaspoon is 5 ml.

TEMPERATURES

	°C	°F	Gas Mark
Very slow	120	250	1
Slow	150	300	2
Mod slow	160	325	3
Moderate	180	350	4
Mod hot	190(g) – 210(e)	375 – 425	5
Hot	200(g) – 240(e)	400 – 475	6
Very hot	230(g) – 260(e)	450 – 525	8

(g) = gas (e) = electric